the value of urban design

A research project commissioned by CABE and DETR

to examine the value added by good urban design

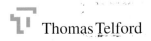
Thomas Telford

cabe

UCL

DETR
ENVIRONMENT
TRANSPORT
REGIONS

Commission for Architecture and the Built Environment

Tower Building

11 York Street

London SE1 7NX

Telephone 020 7960 2400

www.cabe.org.uk

Department of the Environment, Transport and the Regions

Eland House

Bressenden Place

London SW1E 5DU

Telephone 020 7944 3000

www.detr.gov.uk

Further copies of this report are available from:

$\top$ Thomas Telford

The Customer Services Department

Thomas Telford Limited, Units I/K

Paddock Wood Distribution Centre

Paddock Wood, Tonbridge

Kent TN12 6UU

Tel: 020 7665 2464

Fax: 020 7665 2245

www.thomastelford.com

ISBN 07277 2981 0

Design by Kneath Associates

Printed in Great Britain by Latimer Trend

Foreword

THE *Value of Urban Design* asks some fundamental questions about the place of architecture and design in modern society.

In what ways does good design – in this case good urban design– produce economic and social value? What do high quality buildings and spaces give back, in hard financial and utilitarian terms, to those who fund and use them? And how can that value be meaningfully captured so that clients, investors and developers are persuaded that good design adds to the bottom line and gives their product a competitive edge?

This research from the Bartlett, based on a comprehensive literature and research review and case studies of selected mixed-use developments in the UK, begins to answer these questions. Encouragingly, the answers suggest that good design brings very specific economic, social and environmental benefits to a range of stakeholders, for example by improving returns on investments, helping to deliver more lettable area, reducing whole-life costs, increasing workforce productivity and producing a regeneration dividend.

For CABE this is an excellent starting point from which to build up the evidential core of our work. We aim now to cast the net wider than commercial developments and look at capturing the socio-economic value of good design across a range of building types, particularly those in the public sector. We are confident that good design can be shown to bring a variety of benefits, including less crime, a more vibrant public realm, more efficient movement and improved health. All this means less social exclusion and cash savings for the public purse.

The research presented here is not, then, an idle academic exercise. It is intended to form part of a growing resource of information which can underpin investment and development decisions. And from CABE's perspective, it forms part of a hard-nosed effort to ensure that good architecture and design are valued and hence properly funded by all those clients, both public and private, who create the buildings and spaces that form the backdrop to our daily lives.

Sir Stuart Lipton
Chairman
Commission for Architecture and the Built Environment

Sir Stuart Lipton
Chairman
Commission for Architecture and the Built Environment

Research Team

Matthew Carmona

Claudio de Magalhães

Michael Edwards

Bob Awuor

Sherin Aminossehe

Steering Group

Les Sparks	CABE (Chairman)
Robert Bargery	CABE
John Billingham	Urban Design Group
Peter Ellis	DETR
Ziona Strelitz	Ziona Strelitz Associates

Acknowledgements

THANKS are due to the many developers, owners, funding bodies, designers, occupiers, local authority officers and passers-by who agreed to be interviewed. Not all will agree with the assessments of their projects, but it is hoped all will accept the importance of the research and the even-handedness with which it has been undertaken.

Particular thanks go to Dr Tony Key and his colleagues at Investment Property Database (IPD) and to the members of the Steering Group.

Contents

1.0 Report Structure

THIS report is structured to reflect the research process. Section 3 defines the aims and methods of the research. Section 4 outlines the results of the literature and research review. Sections 5 and 6 report on the empirical research findings by presenting the case studies and discussing the views of key stakeholders against the three dimensions of value – economic, social and environmental. Section 7 presents the detailed conclusions of the research and Section 8 makes recommendations for further research.

Key findings are summarised in Section 2, along with recommendations for improving practice.

2.0 Key Findings

GRADUALLY, the case is being made across the development industry that good urban design brings better value. Speaking at the Investment Returns conference hosted by the Royal Institution of Chartered Surveyors in September 2000, Alan Chatham, director of the development company Birmingham Mailbox Ltd, argued that good urban design can increase value several times over by creating what he called 'pitch' – or the opportunity to sell. In that sense, he and others have argued that good urban design has real commercial value.

By means of a literature and research review and case studies of commercial developments, this research sought to test this proposition and ask how the value added by good urban design can be released.

2.1 Good urban design adds value

The research suggested that good urban design adds value by increasing the economic viability of development and by delivering social and environmental benefits.

Good urban design adds economic value by

- producing high returns on investments (good rental returns and enhanced capital values)
- placing developments above local competition at little cost
- responding to occupier demand
- helping to deliver more lettable area (higher densities)
- reducing management, maintenance, energy and security costs
- contributing to more contented and productive workforces
- supporting the 'life giving' mixed-use elements in developments
- creating an urban regeneration and place marketing dividend
- differentiating places and raising their prestige
- opening up investment opportunities, raising confidence in development opportunities and attracting grant monies
- reducing the cost to the public purse of rectifying urban design mistakes.

And good design adds social and environmental value by

- creating well connected, inclusive and accessible new places
- delivering mixed-use environments with a broad range of facilities and amenities available to all
- delivering development sensitive to its context
- enhancing the sense of safety and security within and beyond developments
- returning inaccessible or run down areas and amenities to beneficial public use
- boosting civic pride and enhancing civic image
- creating more energy efficient and less polluting development
- revitalising urban heritage.

The research indicated that the existence of these benefits was increasingly acknowledged across stakeholder groups – by investors, developers, designers, occupiers, public authorities and everyday users.

2.2 Who benefits?

- **Investors** benefit through favourable returns on their investments and through satisfying occupier demand, although the full pay-off may not be immediate.

- **Developers** benefit by attracting investors and pre-lets more easily and hence from enhanced company image. If they retain a stake in their developments for long enough, they also benefit from good returns on their investments.

- **Designers** benefit because good urban design is crucially dependent on their input.

- **Occupiers** benefit from the better performance, loyalty, health and satisfaction of their employees and from the increased prestige that well-designed developments command with guests and clients.

- **Everyday users** and **society as a whole** benefit from the economic advantages of successful regeneration, including new and retained jobs, and also through access to a better quality environment and an enhanced range of amenities and facilities.

- **Public authorities** benefit by meeting their obligation to deliver a well-designed, economically and socially viable environment and often by ripple effects to adjoining areas.

2.3 How can greater value be released?

While the research identified economic, social and environmental benefits flowing from good urban design, it also identified barriers to delivery, particularly those inherent in established patterns of investment and development. Nevertheless, key stakeholders (including investors and occupiers) are increasingly valuing urban design and its perceived (particularly economic) dividends.

In this section, a number of recommendations are made that may – in time – encourage a greater shared valuing of, and investment in, good urban design.

Extending value concerns beyond prestige markets (promoting value)

The message that good urban design does not necessarily cost more to deliver but nevertheless offers strong competitive advantages needs to be spread to those operating across all sectors of the market – and not just at the prestige end. This is a task for CABE, the DETR and local authorities, who might enlist the support of the Urban Design Alliance and representative bodies.

There is still a need to change perceptions about what constitutes good urban design, and to ensure that this extends beyond limited corporate image-making objectives to a more fundamental design responsibility. Occupiers in particular need to be persuaded of the advantages of good urban design since their attitudes influence the actions of developers and investors. This may not be straightforward given the disparate nature of occupier organisations.

Fulfilling the public sector role

The role of the public sector is crucial to the delivery of value through urban design. This role extends far beyond regulatory planning processes, notwithstanding their important role in stopping introspective, exclusive and disconnected developments. Local authorities can and should be proactive, setting the urban design agenda through

- clear development plan policies supported by design briefs, frameworks and masterplans
- using their influence to help ensure that gap funding is conditional on the delivering of good urban design
- using the leverage offered by ownership of brownfield sites (the research revealed that this can be decisive in ensuring better quality urban design)
- working with private interests to achieve agreed economic and urban design objectives

Local authorities must be willing to see high quality urban (and architectural) design as a component of development strategies, including those which are conservation-led. Achieving this may require better publicity to be given to contemporary urban design success stories – nationally and particularly locally.

Educating for better urban design

The research indicated that poor quality urban design is not necessarily a result either of an active decision not to invest in good urban design or of a lack of time and effort put into producing a high quality product. In their own way, all the case study developments were carefully designed and crafted products. In the better ones, though, urban design considerations extended beyond corporate image-making objectives.

Poor delivery, where it occurs, often results in part from a lack of urban design skills in both the private and public sectors. Efforts are already being made by the DETR and CABE to address this skills deficit. Fundamentally, the gap needs to be filled across all professional education concerned with the built environment (particularly in the finance/investment related professions) and through continuing professional development. Initiatives on this front cannot come too soon.

Delivering better urban design

As well as these 'process' related recommendations, the research revealed a number of findings that might usefully inform urban design practice.

- Delivering good urban design seems to some extent to rely on delivering the **critical mass** needed to support it. New public spaces, infrastructure improvements, mixing uses and so forth all rely on the realisation of developments large enough to fund their delivery. This suggests an important role for the public sector in assembling larger sites.

- Smaller development can contribute to the delivery of good urban design if clear arrangements and strategies are put in place (by public or private parties) to **coordinate adjoining sites** and help deliver a well-considered and coherent whole. Proactive planning is the key.

- **Lifetime costs** should be considered upfront in the development process. This is easier said than done when many of those with a longer term interest in developments do not come on board until later in the development process. Nevertheless, the capacity of good urban design to reduce management and maintenance costs should be highlighted.

- Where the **strategic dimension of urban design** is appreciated and acted upon through positive planning at a larger spatial scale – particularly the integration of development into established infrastructure – the value (particularly social value) added by development is enhanced.

- **Mixing uses** leads directly to higher user and occupier satisfaction and was fundamental to the social, economic and environmental value added by the most successful case studies.

- **Public spaces and amenities** function far more successfully if located at accessible, well-connected points in developments.

- Good urban design can make areas more attractive to higher income residents and the businesses and services that supply or employ them. It is important, however, to **sustain social diversity** within new developments to help ensure that the benefits of regeneration are widely shared.

3.0 The Research

3.1 The research background

ALTHOUGH a small body of national and international research has examined the issue of design and value (see Section 4), this remains a neglected yet significant area in the built environment research agenda.

It is also a complex one. Definitive answers about the value of urban design are difficult to provide, given variations in contextual and market conditions and differences between investment sectors. To come close to definitive answers, complex methodologies are likely to be required. And answers are likely to be no less complex, making dissemination to a wide range of audiences difficult. Adding to the complexity is the simple fact that design constitutes just one influence on economic value; location, use, market and usable floor area will also be significant.

At the outset of the research, all parties were under no illusions that simple answers to the deceptively simple question 'Does urban design add value?' may not be possible. As American research on the economics of architectural and urban design has indicated, value is added in some circumstances and contexts but not in others (Vandell & Lane, 1989).

In the UK, the context within which decisions on design and development are made has changed over the past five years:

- a renewed concern for design (particularly urban design) is apparent within the planning process

- the Urban Task Force report has shown that urban design can play an important role in regeneration

- developers have shown a renewed interest in the part good design can play in the development process

- CABE has been set up partly to champion the cause of good urban design.

As a consequence, it becomes all the more important to be precise about the part that good urban design can play in realising economic, social and environmental objectives.

3.2 Research aims and key questions

The aim of the research was

> *to identify and where possible measure the value added by good urban design, and to demonstrate the benefits that flow from well-designed urban space.*

The key research questions were:

- Does better urban design add value and if so how?

- Who benefits?

- How can greater value be released?

3.3 Research method

A three-stage methodology was adopted.

Stage 1 – literature and research review

The review encompassed literature and research on the value of urban design and the value of good design in related fields (architecture, conservation, sustainable development, etc.). As well as examining the nature of value and its relation to development, design and policy, the review enabled the development of a series of research tools:

- a working conceptualisation of urban design – to reflect the broad scope of the discipline and to delimit the research efforts

- an analytical tool – as a means to appraise the urban design qualities of the case studies

- a value identification and listing (economic, social and environmental) to identify a range of costs and benefits for investigation through the case studies

- an assessment of the range of stakeholders involved in the process and the value that theoretically accrues to each

- an analytical framework to structure the case studies.

Stage 2 – case studies

The case studies formed the empirical heart of the research. The work encompassed

- the identification of case study developments, reflecting a range of commercial contexts and approaches to urban design

- urban design analysis of each case study by the research team (see Annex B)

- detailed interviews with key stakeholders to gauge their perceptions of the economic, social and environmental value of good urban design (see Annex C)

- eliciting information on development costs and on expected and actual returns on investments (see Annex C)

- a synthesis of the qualitative and quantitative data to gauge performance of the case study developments and assess whether the benefits of good urban design can be incorporated into the expectations and practices of decision-makers.

Stage 3 – synthesis and dissemination

The final stage of the research continued the process of synthesis by adding the results of the case studies to those of the literature and research review. Initial research questions were revisited and consideration given to how research on the value of urban design could be taken forward.

4.0 Literature and Research Review

4.1 Questions on value and urban design

TO structure the literature and research review, the following questions were asked about the nature of value and its relationship to urban design:

■ What is meant by value?

■ Why does value matter?

■ What are the lessons from history?

■ What is meant by good urban design?

■ How do perceptions of good design change?

■ How can the value and quality of urban design be measured?

■ What might be the value of good urban design?

■ Who incurs the costs and receives the benefits of good urban design?

■ What are the barriers to realising enhanced design value?

The following discussion overviews the key outcomes of this exercise, but does not represent the full literature/research review undertaken for the project. The Bibliography should be consulted for the full range of sources used. Annex A discusses in greater detail the methodological approaches adopted for some existing research projects.

4.2 What is meant by value?

Literally defined, value is a measure of the worth of something to its owner or any other person who derives benefit from it, this being the amount at which it can be exchanged. Two concepts of value have been distinguished in economics: 'value in use' (the pleasure a commodity – as a good or service – generates for its owner or user) and 'value in exchange' (the quantity of other commodities – or more usually money – a commodity can be swapped for).

Urban design has been widely considered to have the potential to generate benefits for built environment stakeholders (Parfect & Power, 1997; Worpole, 1999). However, while the direct benefits to stakeholders (in the form of enhanced real estate asset value) can be evaluated through their monetary 'exchange value' in the marketplace using standard valuation techniques, the same cannot be said of the wider 'value in use' benefits that accrue to society as a whole (Eccles, 1996). This is perhaps inevitable given that standard valuation techniques, being concerned solely with value in a market situation, exclude concepts of social value, aesthetic value and other non-market concepts of worth (Britton, 1989).

It is an established assumption in economic analysis that the benefits of most goods and services accrue to those who pay for them and are not extended to a wider group. The exchange value of a good or service is therefore indicated by the price at which it is traded in the market. But market prices are poor indicators of the value of many collective public benefits since their key feature consists of externalities which are not taken into account in the price for which the goods are sold. Thus, for example, the social benefits of a high quality public realm and the productivity gains arising from well-designed urban spaces and workplaces occur in the form of externalities. This is a distinctive characteristic of 'public goods' that have no immediately identifiable monetary exchange value and are therefore not usually considered important by the market. Such goods can easily be undervalued in public and private investment decisions. Yet their true value can be much greater than the supply price or the cost incurred in making them available.

4.3 Why does value matter?

The increasing prominence of the sustainability agenda has brought to the fore the issue of how the urban environment should be organised, how it should be managed and how large should be its 'ecological footprint'. At the same time the pressures of inter-city competition for jobs and economic activities in a globalised economy have forced the planning and urban policy community to pay greater attention to the contribution that well-designed and managed urban environments might make towards enhancing the economic competitiveness of places (Urban Task Force, 1999).

The result has been the renewed focusing of attention on the quality of the urban environment and the process through which better quality can be produced and maintained. In the context of a diminishing role for the public sector in the direct provision of buildings and public spaces, the focus of that attention has been on the outcomes of largely private sector led development processes.

Demonstrating the value of good urban design, or assessing its costs and benefits (in aesthetic, environmental, health, safety, economic and cultural terms) is part of the effort to link design quality to the decision-making logic of private sector development interests. The other side of the coin is the need to develop an understanding of how the public sector can modify the institutional barriers and regulatory context in which decisions about design are made, eliminating legal and institutional barriers to good design and introducing incentives to encourage its delivery.

Regrettably, commercial pressures often militate against long-term investment in design quality. The problem is compounded because decisions regarding the built environment are often made by those far removed from their impact on the ground – by investment fund managers, company head offices, commercial development firms, statutory undertakers and so forth, as well as in the public sector by stakeholders who do not regard themselves as designers at all – by politicians, district surveyors, housing managers and accountants (see Section 4.10).

Thus the argument of a former Secretary of State for the Environment (Gummer, 1994) that investors in the built environment should show a sense of civic responsibility could only carry so far. Exhortations of the public benefits of good design will have a limited impact in a climate where financial value and return is viewed as the primary measure of success for private sector investment. Similarly, attempts by central government, local authorities and CABE's predecessor the Royal Fine Art Commission to raise the standard of design through persuasion, demonstration and even intervention have come and gone, usually without inspiring a significant improvement in the general standard of development. In part this is because development interests have yet fully to embrace the message.

To compound the problem, urban design has all too often fallen through the gaps left between individual professional responsibilities. Only, it seems, by offering solid evidence that good urban design can deliver better value (social and environmental, but particularly economic) will sceptical minds be turned. By placing better urban design on the positive side of the balance sheet, a change in private as well as public investment decisions might be secured.

4.4 What are the lessons from history?

Some of the most highly valued parts of our cities are instances of good urban design, areas which have delivered good investment returns and an attractive built environment over decades or even centuries. The great landed estates of central London are the most significant 'modern' examples – modern in the sense that they were the product of contractual relationships between landowners, builders and users of the kind still made today. These areas, such as Belgravia, Marylebone and Bloomsbury, show how an investment in good masterplanning, systematic regulation (but not total standardisation) of building design and the strategic placing of urban spaces can produce both enduring use values and lasting streams of profits, rents and capital value growth for owners (Summerson, 1978).

In a later period – the early twentieth century – many garden suburbs in Britain, Germany and elsewhere have had the same impact. Although individual buildings may be very variable in quality, the ensemble has been maintained and valued by occupiers and owners alike, often generating fierce protective loyalty in residents. Hampstead Garden Suburb is the best-known example, but others include Bedford Park in London and Selly Park in Birmingham. On a larger scale, some new towns are enduring equally well.

One of the crucial elements in the success of all these examples is scale. Developments were laid out in large enough ownership units to enable the initial promoter to capture (in higher rents and prices) most of the benefits created through good design and high quality public space. In economic jargon, the externalities were internalised within the scheme. The survival and the self-maintaining quality of many of these localities have been helped by the leasehold structure of tenure which meant that the ground landlord had an incentive to maintain the quality in the long-run – and to do so through reinvestment and through the lease conditions imposed on leaseholders. (In doing this, the landlord also protected the interests of the leaseholder.) Only where the leasehold system failed and the area's quality was left to the uncoordinated action of freeholders or the fitful action of public authorities did the quality break down. Somers Town, built in the late eighteenth century on land sold by Lord Somers beside Euston and St Pancras stations in London, is a good example of this failure (Clarke, 1992).

It is, however, not only through large-scale leasehold development that good urban design has been created. Many cities have large areas which were first developed in more piecemeal ways, but which survive and continue to generate value today – both use value for citizens and market value for owners. Hebbert (1998) has shown how well many such areas have survived in London, often confounding the intentions of later planners.

The key to their survival has tended to be the existence of good functional and adaptable street systems and flexibility in the uses to which the building stock can be put, and therefore a responsiveness to the changing needs of users and of markets. An interesting example is Camden Town in London, often scheduled for redevelopment but surviving and thriving largely intact today. The key ingredients of success here include the existence of well-proportioned and interesting street axes, a visually rich and functional layout and the existence of 'backland' and flexible building structures into which commercial activity could grow.

This brief review of historical examples indicates how a set of often simple urban design principles can combine with social and economic circumstances to deliver lasting value to investors, occupiers and society. Clearly the development context is different today from when many of these investments were conceived and realised, not least in the move towards a more short-term investment culture. Nevertheless, the market truism remains the same, that investors seeking profit will favour those forms of development perceived to deliver the highest returns on their investment. Thus, if it can be demonstrated that good urban design pays dividends, then investment in high quality design will be far more likely to follow.

4.5 What is meant by good urban design?

Two immediate problems are faced by research concerned with the design of the built environment. First, how to define the exact scope and nature of good design – in this case good urban design – and second, how to make objective judgements about the relative merits or otherwise of particular design solutions. As a starting point, it is important to have some overall concept of what constitutes good design to provide a basis on which to make informed judgements.

Definitions of urban design are many and various. Perhaps the simplest of recent definitions is quoted by Cowan (2000) as 'the art of making places'. The most significant, however, is found in Planning Policy Guidance Note 1 (PPG1), representing an attempt by central government to define the scope of the subject area. It states that

> *"... urban design should be taken to mean the relationship between different buildings; the relationship between buildings and the streets, squares, parks and waterways and other spaces which make up the public domain; the nature and quality of the public domain itself; the relationship of one part of a village, town or city with other parts; and the patterns of movement and activity which are thereby established: in short, the complex relationships between all the elements of built and unbuilt space"*
> (DoE, 1997, para. 14).

On this definition, urban design is concerned with

■ all the constituent physical parts of the built environment to which the public have access

■ the way these parts fit together to create networks of space and activity

■ the functioning of those space networks

■ their role as a social venue.

Of greater value than simple definitions are the numerous attempts to synthesise the traditions of urban design into usable comprehensive frameworks (Bentley et al, 1985; Tibbalds, 1988; Urban Design Group, 1994). Common to many recent conceptualisations is the notion that urban design encompasses much more than the visual impact of buildings and space: social, environmental and functional dimensions must be considered alongside visual or urban form-based concerns. And urban design must be viewed as a process as well a product-based discipline.

By Design (DETR and CABE, 2000) draws from a broad range of literature to make the case that 'successful streets, spaces, villages, towns and cities tend to have characteristics in common'. These are encapsulated in the following 'objectives of urban design':

- **Character** – to promote character in townscape and landscape by responding to and reinforcing locally distinctive patterns of development and culture.

- **Continuity and Enclosure** – to promote the continuity of street frontages and the enclosure of space by development which clearly defines private and public areas.

- **Quality of the Public Realm** – to promote public spaces and routes that are attractive, safe, uncluttered and work effectively for all in society, including disabled and elderly people.

- **Ease of Movement** – to promote accessibility and local permeability by making places that connect with each other and are easy to move through, putting people before traffic and integrating land uses and transport.

- **Legibility** – to promote legibility through development that provides recognisable routes, intersections and landmarks to help people find their way around.

- **Adaptability** – to promote adaptability through development that can respond to changing social, technological and economic conditions.

- **Diversity** – to promote diversity and choice through a mix of compatible developments and uses that work together to create viable places that respond to local needs.

Because of their emergence out of extensive research and debate and their inclusion in government guidance, these seven objectives carry considerable legitimacy. They are useful because they suggest clear, objective attributes against which success in urban design can be assessed. They also imply that there is such a thing as a 'public' view on what constitutes good urban design. Such arguments have long been put forward by such influential writers as Christopher Alexander (1977) and Kevin Lynch (1960). Finally, the set of objectives provides a broadly accepted conceptualisation of urban design that the current research could adopt as a basis for evaluating the case study developments.

4.6 How do perceptions of good design differ?

Research has consistently shown that planners, local politicians, the public and architects have very different perceptions of architectural design (Jeffrey & Reynolds, 1999). Although similar research on perceptions of urban design has not yet been undertaken, it is likely that these too will differ. Many stakeholders are involved in making, using and managing urban developments. Drawing from a range of sources (Lock, 1993; Adams, 1994; Lang, 1994; RICS & DoE, 1996; Guy, 1998), Table 1 lists each of these groups' primary motivations and how they typically impact on perceptions of urban design.

Views on what constitutes good design in the built environment will vary between stakeholders and will depend on the audience perceiving them rather than on the exact nature of the development. Thus an office worker or shopper may have a very different perception of what makes a good urban environment from an estate manager charged with

Table 1: Stakeholders and their Motivations

Stakeholder (commercial property)	Primary Motivations	Concern for Better Urban Design
1. Private Interests		
Landowners	Maximising returns	Only in-so-far that profits are not diminished and other holdings are protected
Funders (short-term)	Good financial security, risk against return	Only if higher risk is balanced by a higher return
Developers	Buildable, marketable, profitable, quickly delivered,	If better urban design adds to either marketability or profitability
Design professionals	Meets brief, satisfies client, individually designed, innovative	Depends on training, but too often concerned for building design at the expense of urban design
Investors (long-term)	Good liquidity, easy/cost effective to maintain, profitable over the long-term	If a market exists and therefore if design adds to profits and reduces running costs over time
Management agents	Management efficiency	Only that increased costs are reflected in higher fees
Occupiers	Value for money, flexible, secure, functional, correct image	In-so-far as better urban design creates a more efficient work environment and is affordable
2. Public Interests		
Planning authorities	Protects local amenities, meets planning policies, respects broad public interest, low environmental impact	Highly concerned, but frequently unable to articulate requirements or concerned to the extent that wider economic and social goals are not compromised
Highways authorities	Safe, efficient, adoptable (roads)	As long as functional requirements are met first
Fire and emergency services	Accessible in emergencies	Little direct concern
Police authority	Designed to prevent crime	As far as better design improves image and reduces crime
Building control	Designed to protect public safety	Little direct concern
3. Community Interests		
Amenity groups	Contextually compatible in design and uses	Highly concerned, but often broadly conservative in outlook
Local communities	Reflecting local preferences and protecting property values	Highly concerned but would often prefer no development at all

its upkeep, whilst a developer may perceive the added value in a development very differently from a local resident. These differing perceptions needed to be reflected in the research by interviewing all the key stakeholders involved in each case study.

The activity of urban design, then, needs to reconcile a set of often very different private and public aspirations. If the private aspiration necessarily tends to be chiefly one of economic viability, the public aspiration is one of social equity in which key public objectives are met through the development process. Economic viability is the first and foremost form of overarching value. But the social benefits that developments deliver provide a second form.

Economic and social value are complemented by a further, less readily apparent but still highly significant, dimension of overarching value, namely the environmental value generated by more ecologically responsible patterns of development. As environmental concerns do not contribute directly to day to day user experience of developments, neither their 'exchange value' nor their 'value in use' is readily apparent. The tendency has therefore been to marginalise them. They have, however, been increasingly stressed in recent urban design literature (Lang, 1994; Frey, 1999; Rudlin & Falk, 1999) and were central to the 'framework of design principles for creating more liveable places' identified by the Urban Task Force (1999, pp 70–71).

These three overarching forms of value, along with the seven urban design objectives identified by the DETR and CABE, extend the limited notion of 'exchange value' to one of 'sustainable value'.

Figure 1: Urban Design Objectives and Overarching Sustainable Value

SUSTAINABLE VALUES

URBAN DESIGN OBJECTIVES	A. Economic viability	B. Social benefit	C. Environmental support
1. character			
2. continuity and enclosure			
2. quality of the public realm			
4. ease of movement			
5. legibility			
6. adaptability			
7. diversity			

Economic viability – development that is economically feasible and which remains economically viable over the long-term.

Social benefit – development that responds to broader public objectives and concerns and which as far as possible benefits from the support of the local community in which it sits.

Environmental support – development that delivers more energy efficient, robust, ecologically supportive and less polluting patterns of urban form.

4.7 How can the value and quality of urban design be measured?

Value

The relevant literature shows two basic approaches (not necessarily mutually exclusive) to measuring the value of design. The first is a mainly qualitative treatment (RICS & DoE, 1996; Verhage & Needham, 1997; Guy, 1998; Loe, 1999; Worpole, 1999) which focuses on how the value of good design is perceived by the various stakeholders involved in the production and use of urban space, how this perception relates to design-related decision-making processes and how policy influences the outcomes of those decisions.

The second is a quantitative, econometric treatment (Vandell & Lane, 1989; Doiron et al, 1992; DNH et al, 1996; Eppli & Tu, 1999; Property Council of Australia, 1999). The focus is on measuring the value – or more specifically the costs and benefits – generated by given levels of design quality so as to inform the financial decisions of stakeholders. Key issues concern how to convert intangible benefits and costs of design quality into monetary values, the definition of temporal limits for such calculations, the distribution of costs and benefits amongst stakeholders and how these accrue over time. In such cases, assessing value normally means converting its various components into prices, which can then be compared and benefits offset against costs.

Both qualitative and quantitative techniques come up against conceptual and practical difficulties, which include:

- the problem of defining urban design on simple scales from good to bad, and within that coping with the fact that urban design is both a product and a process

- the problem that good urban design – even more than good architectural design – generates benefits for adjoining sites and areas; therefore only a proportion of the benefit created by good urban design is enjoyed by those working in a particular development or visiting it as customers

- even those benefits enjoyed by workers and customers may not be transmitted as profits to companies, to the rents paid by occupiers, or to the valuations placed on buildings by investors

- different stakeholders have different expectations regarding value.

The current research included a qualitative appreciation of how different stakeholders perceive the value of good urban design and used evidence from quantitative indicators of commercial success where available.

Quality

Although perceptions about the exact nature of good design vary, judgements still need to be made about the relative success or otherwise of particular urban design solutions and their impact on economic, social and environmental value. To do this, it was necessary to consider how quality in urban design might be measured and recorded.

Recent attempts to measure urban design quality are discussed in Annex A. Among them are UK research projects supported by the RICS & DoE (1996), a study by the Property

Council of Australia (1999) and Vandell & Lane's work in the USA (1989). The UK research developed a sophisticated assessment tool through which developments were measured against 50 urban design attributes under four broad headings (see Table 2). Assessment was largely undertaken by members of the research team, supplemented by discussions with some of the stakeholders involved in each development. The tool provided a means to develop more objective assessments of design quality, by turning the attributes into quantitative values on a scale of 0 to 4 – the final outcome being an average rating for each of the five developments assessed.

Table 2: Design Assessment Criteria

Research	Categories/Criteria
RICS & DoE, 1996	1. Functional and social use (12 criteria)
	2. Natural environment and sustainability (11 criteria)
	3. Visual (12 criteria)
	4. The urban experience (15 criteria)
Property Council of Australia, 1999	1. Degree of 'community equity', measured in public space design, of amenity quality, area accessibility and vitality, and diversity
	2. Level of environmental performance, measured in terms of climatic responsiveness, and other environmental and sustainability indicators
	3. Responsiveness to qualities of the urban context and landscape, and to historical characteristics
	4. Relevance to present and future, measured through the degree of purposeful innovation
	5. Ability to change over time
	6. Impact on public life and community perception
	7. Professional excellence in inputs such as development concept, planning, architecture and design, facility management and development upkeep
Vandell & Lane, 1989	1. Qualities of materials used in the exterior skin
	2. Fenestration: composition and scale of the façade
	3. Massing: compositional bulk and volumetrics of the building
	4. Design of interior public space: design of lobby plus other interior public space
	5. View on skyline: as seen from a distance
	6. Design of exterior public spaces
	7. Responsiveness to neighbourhood: relationship to abutting uses
	8. Provision of public amenities

In the Australian research, a nationwide call for nominations of examples of good urban design ensured that some subjective judgement was made by those nominating developments. A four person team drawn from different professions assessed the nominated developments against seven criteria to select the best-designed schemes.

In the American study, a much larger sample of 102 office buildings in Boston and Cambridge, Massachusetts, was selected for analysis, with design quality assessment based purely on aesthetics. Eighty architects were asked to make an initial evaluation and a smaller number completed the task, rating buildings across a 0 to 5 range, the outcome being a mean rating for each building and a standard deviation.

The assessment methodology for the present research adopted characteristics of each of these studies. The first requirement was transparency, achieved by establishing clear criteria against which judgements on urban design quality could be made. A second requirement was a shared acceptance of the principles adopted, achieved in this case by basing assessment on principles established in government guidance. A third requirement was objectivity, a clear characteristic of the scoring systems adopted for the RICS/DoE research and the American work.

Objectivity needed to be accompanied by a further characteristic – inclusiveness. Those responsible for producing and using environments needed to be involved in making judgements about quality. To make that possible, simplicity was also necessary.

To avoid simply recording design characteristics, each development was measured against a set of urban design performance criteria and given a mark for how successfully it was judged to have met them (see Figure 2).

Figure 2: Urban Design Analysis Tool

Case Study . . . . Assessor . . . . Occupation . . . .

Urban Design Objectives	Performance Criteria	Strengths	Weaknesses	Evaluation 0 = not at all successful 5 = very successful
1 Character	A distinct sense of place responding to local context			0 1 2 3 4 5
2 Continuity and Enclosure	Continuity of frontages and clearly defined public space			0 1 2 3 4 5
3 Quality of the Public Realm	Safe, attractive and functional public space			0 1 2 3 4 5
4 Ease of Movement	An accessible, well connected, pedestrian friendly environment			0 1 2 3 4 5
5 Legibility	A readily understandable, easily navigable environment			0 1 2 3 4 5
6 Adaptability	Flexible and adaptable public and private environments			0 1 2 3 4 5
7 Diversity	A varied environment offering a range of uses and experiences			0 1 2 3 4 5
Summary:				Total Rating

Note: Developments featuring good urban design should rate well on all counts. Nevertheless, the total rating – out of 35 – provides some indication of overall urban design quality.

4.8 How might good urban design add value?

Good urban design can confer two distinct forms of benefits. Direct benefits (usually economic) accrue to those responsible for investing in development (whether from the public or private sectors). Indirect benefits (social but also environmental) accrue to others and to society at large. As noted above (see Section 4.2), these two forms of value can be further distinguished between value that has tangible financial consequences and can be measured through monetary worth (exchange value) and value that is more intangible and does not lend itself to direct financial measurement (value in use). Such value is no less real but is not usually reflected in simple valuation techniques. In the housing sector, for example, the Urban Villages Forum (1995, p1) have argued that conventional concepts of value for money associated with mass housing fail to consider the social costs of poor health, crime, commuting and so forth – costs that eventually fall on the public purse.

Unfortunately, the relationship between design and value is unlikely to be a straightforward correlation between better design and increased value. While in certain respects good design may increase value, in others it may increase costs, at least in the short term. Such costs may or may not be compensated for by the increases in value.

The potential components of value generated through good design are presented in Table 3 and a similar table for costs is presented in Table 4. The tables illustrate the wide range of financially tangible concerns, but also the range of intangible considerations that nevertheless impact on any assessment of costs and values in urban design. They furthermore demonstrate the wide range of economic as opposed to social and environmental values and costs, and the difficulty in measuring social and environmental (and even full economic) value through simple financial means.

4.9 Who incurs the costs and receives the benefits of good urban design?

"The market required to support a potential development consists of the population seeking services and their capacity to pay for them. The question the developer must ask is: 'Is the market large enough to support this development?' The question the public sector asks is: 'How is the public interest to be furthered by this development?'" (Lang, 1994, p375).

Table 3: The Potential Value of Good Urban Design

	Economic Value	Social Value	Environmental Value
Financial Tangibles	■ Potential for higher land values ■ Higher sale values ■ Increased funding potential (public and private) ■ Higher rental returns ■ Increased asset value (on which to borrow) ■ Reduced running costs ■ Maintenance of value/income ■ Reduced maintenance costs (over life) ■ Better re-sale values ■ Easy maintenance if high quality materials ■ Reduced security expenditure ■ Reduced running costs (energy usage) ■ Reduced public expenditure (on health care/crime prevention/urban management and maintenance) ■ Increased economic viability for neighbouring uses/opportunities ■ Increased local tax revenue ■ Reduced travel costs	■ Regenerative potential (encouraging other development) ■ Better security and less crime ■ Less pollution (better health) ■ Higher property prices ■ Less stress (better health) ■ Reduced travel costs	■ Reduced energy consumption ■ Reduced resource/land consumption
Financial Intangibles	■ Potential for greater security of investment depending on market ■ Quicker permissions (reduced cost, less uncertainty) ■ Distinctiveness (greater product differentiation) ■ Allows difficult sites to be tackled ■ Better developer reputation (increased confidence/ 'trademark' value) ■ Future collaborations more likely ■ Enhanced design professional reputation ■ Increased workload and repeat commissions from high quality, stable clients ■ Competitive investment edge ■ Higher quality longer term tenants ■ Happier workforce (better recruiting and retention) ■ Better productivity ■ Increased business (client) confidence ■ Fewer disruptive moves ■ Increased occupier prestige ■ Increased city marketing potential	■ Reduced public/private discord (more time for positive planning) ■ Greater accessibility to other uses/facilities ■ Increased public support (less opposition) ■ Increased cultural vitality ■ Better quality of life ■ More inclusive public space ■ A more equitable/accessible environment ■ Greater civic pride (sense of community) ■ Reinforced sense of place	■ Less environmental damage ■ An ecologically diverse and supportive environment

Table 4: The Potential Costs of Good Urban Design

	Economic Costs	Social Costs	Environmental Costs
Financial Tangibles	■ Potential for reduced land values ■ Higher risk if increased development costs ■ Higher infrastructure costs (public space and social infrastructure) ■ Higher construction costs ■ Higher design costs (professional fees) ■ Greater capital investment ■ Continued private sector responsibility for public/private spaces ■ Higher rents ■ Higher management fees	■ Higher public investment in design – planning advice, guidance, award schemes, etc.	■ None
Financial Intangibles	■ Increased design time (not always recognised in fees) ■ More complex management if mixed use development	■ Risk of no development if design standards demanded are too high ■ Prospect of gentrification	■ None

When client expectations are met without negative impact on the interests of other stakeholders in an area or on the environment, development might be regarded as a success. Nevertheless, good urban design offers the opportunity to give something to community and public interests as well as to private promoters of schemes. Urban design, like architecture, is a public activity, with impacts felt in the public sphere and often well beyond the site boundaries. However, the nature of development as perceived by the private and public sectors differs greatly.

The public sector primarily sees development as a way of furthering the public interest – raising local tax revenues, creating other investment opportunities and supporting public services and those sectors of society poorly served by the market. The private sector is broadly influenced by the demand for particular forms of accommodation, the cost and availability of financing, by the physical structure of the environment and by the ability to secure all the necessary regulatory approvals without undue delay. For them, the marketplace is an uncertain place and development is a risky business (Lang, 1994).

These different perspectives on value are illustrated in a recent analysis of US West Coast downtown commercial developments incorporating new 'public' open space (Loukaitou-Sideris & Banerjee, 1998). The authors argue that the result of divorcing economic viability from social benefits has been the creation of unrelated, inward-looking, self-sufficient, exclusionary, stage-set urban spaces. Thus few of the new commercial developments they surveyed included spaces conceived of as 'public' and most actively excluded sections of society perceived not to 'fit in'.

Crudely, the public sector tends to have long-term goals. Many of the stakeholders in the private sector have shorter time horizons. In part, this is because much of the debate over financing urban design projects comes down to the interplay between two basic fiscal concerns – capital costs and operating costs.

The former is a main concern of all private sector parties, while the latter is easily neglected in the effort to make development happen and extract short-term profits at least equal to those available though less risky investments, for example gilts and equities (Lang, 1994, p379). Furthermore, as finance for commercial projects becomes less and less localised, with often international teams of investors and advisers (including designers) making developments happen, judgements on the viability of projects and the part design plays in this can become increasingly divorced from site-specific and cultural contexts. The potential to demonstrate whether urban design adds value over both the short and long term thus becomes highly significant. Drawing from the values and costs identified in Tables 3 and 4, Table 5 indicates both to whom (in theory) the value of good urban design accrues and over what period. Table 6 repeats the exercise for costs.

The tables suggest that for good urban design to be valued by all stakeholders, it needs to offer distinct dividends over the short as well as the long term – or, alternatively, that the interests of development stakeholders need to be maintained until longer term value is released.

Table 5: The Beneficiaries of Value in Urban Design

Stakeholders	Short-Term Value (social, economic and environmental)	Long-Term Value (social, economic and environmental)
Landowners	Potential for increased land values	
Funders (short term)	Potential for greater security of investment depending on market	
Developers	Quicker permissions (reduced cost, less uncertainty) Increased public support (less opposition) Higher sales values (profitability) Distinctiveness (greater product differentiation) Increased funding potential (public/private) Allows difficult sites to be tackled	Better reputation (increased confidence/'trademark' value) Future collaborations more likely
Design professionals	Increased workload and repeat commissions from high quality, stable clients	Enhanced professional reputation
Investors (long term)	Higher rental returns Increased asset value (on which to borrow) Reduced running costs Competitive investment edge	Maintenance of value/income Reduced maintenance costs (over life) Better re-sale values Higher quality longer term tenants
Management agents		Easy maintenance if high quality materials
Occupiers		Happier workforce (better recruiting and retention) Better productivity Increased business (client) confidence Fewer disruptive moves Greater accessibility to other uses/facilities Reduced security expenditure Increased occupier prestige Reduced running cost (energy usage)
Public Interests (from Table 1)	Regenerative potential (encouraging other development) Reduced public/private discord	Reduced public expenditure (on crime prevention/urban management/urban maintenance/health) More time for positive planning Increased economic viability for neighbouring uses/development opportunities Increased local tax revenue More sustainable environment
Community Interests (from Table 2)		Better security and less crime Increased cultural vitality Less pollution (better health) Less stress (better health) Better quality of life More inclusive public space A more equitable/accessible environment Greater civic pride (sense of community) Reinforced sense of place Higher property prices

Table 6: Meeting the Costs of Good Urban Design

Stakeholders	Long-Term Costs (social, economic and environmental)	Long-Term Costs (social, economic and environmental)
Landowners	Potential for reduced land values	
Funders (short term)	Higher risk through increased development costs Higher infrastructure costs (public space and social infrastructure)	
Developers	Higher construction costs Higher design costs	
Design professionals	Increased design time (not always recognised in fees)	
Investors (long term)		Greater capital investment Continued private sector responsibility for public/private spaces
Management agents		More complex management if mixed use development
Occupiers		Higher rents Higher management fees Higher commercial rates
Public Interests (from Table 1)	Higher public investment in design – planning advice, guidance, award schemes, etc.	Risk of no development if design standards demanded are too high
Community Interests (from Table 2)		Socially exclusive development

4.10 What are the barriers to realising enhanced design value?

Measuring the 'value added' by good urban design is only ever likely to be a staging post to delivering good design, given the various barriers to delivery. Understanding what these barriers are formed an important part of the research.

Table 7: Design Decision-making – Key Factors (after RICS & DoE, 1996)

Stakeholder	Key Factors
Developers	1. Investor and occupier requirements, preferences and tastes, reflected in the prices they are prepared to pay for having those met
	2. The need for flexibility to meet changing circumstances in a market characterised by cyclical behaviour and a slow production process which ties up high levels of capital value
	3. The need to have a product that can be built with available technical and

financial resources, within acceptable time limits, and which will provide adequate levels of financial return

4. The visual characteristics of the development for selling or letting, which will depend on the demand the development needs to cater for, on general perceptions of particular locations (e.g. the need to create a new 'address' through differentiated image), on cultural factors and on the overall situation of the property market

5. The occupation and running cost of developments, which may influence sales and lettings

6. The timing of the development in relation to the stages in the property cycle, which will determine the range of alternative choices open to investors and occupiers and, therefore, the degree to which success will depend on the image or intrinsic qualities of the development

7. The perceived role of design elements and 'image' in smoothing out possible conflicts in negotiations with planning authorities, and in attracting public support. This is related to the need to reduce uncertainty and delay in obtaining planning permission

Investors

1. The rates of return of the investment, in rents and capital value

2. The acceptance of a property to 'good' potential tenants, i.e. those with good credit ratings

3. The capacity of a property to be adaptable to the needs of a variety of 'good' tenants, in the present and in the future, therefore securing a continuous rent flow

4. The acceptance of a property to other investors, which determines if a property can be re-sold to a buyer with a similar view of the investment. This means that design quality needs to reflect directly in the investment performance over its life and at the point of sale

5. The state and prospects of the investment market: economic stability and strong competition in the market favour value added by design. In the short term, good design contributes towards 'product differentiation' and therefore gives the development an edge. In the long term, good design might mean better investment performance and better re-sale prices (Vandell and Lane, 1989; Property Council of Australia, 1999). A weak or unstable market militates against extra investment in quality as it might not be recoverable

6. The state and prospects of the occupancy market: this is linked to the likely demand for design quality from occupiers. As the late 1980s/early 1990s period showed, in an over-supplied market with falling rents, properties of above-average quality will stand a better chance of being leased out to good tenants. In an under-supplied market, with little choice for occupiers, within certain limits any average-quality property will perform well

7. The ability to manage the environment in which the investment is located. This is related to the investors' ability or otherwise to limit the impact of negative externalities, and convert positive ones in financial returns

Occupiers

1. Location in relation to accessibility to markets, consumers, suppliers, transport links, etc.

2. Occupation costs, including rents and running costs, the relative importance of which will vary with the dynamics of the rental markets, energy needs, etc. (e.g. low rents might bring high running costs to the fore and vice versa)

3. Functionality, which refers to the capacity of the property to accommodate with minimum friction the required technological infrastructure, work and management practices and preferably contribute to increased productivity

4. Image, or the ability of a property to express adequately the corporate 'identity' of a firm

5. Physical flexibility, as a dynamic counterpoint to 'functionality'. The property should be able to accommodate – with minimum friction – changes in infrastructure networks, management and work practices

6. The pattern of, and relationship between, staff and the organisation. Research suggests that well-designed environments can help to retain key staff, facilitate recruitment of new staff, improve relationships within the workplace and even improve corporate 'spirit' (Duffy, 1999)

7. The potential for design to improve the productivity of the core business through influencing staff well-being and efficiency, better use of space resources, reduction in occupation costs or better and more efficient links with consumers, suppliers and the outside world in general

The barriers to the realisation of enhanced design value will vary for different stakeholders, just as the rationale for investing in design quality will be different for, say, developers, occupiers or public authorities. They will also vary locally as development contexts, markets and political frameworks and resources change. Nevertheless, a number of key recurring barriers can be identified:

■ **Low awareness** of urban design issues amongst investors and occupiers, relating to how important they see design quality to the success of their operations. Research suggests that different sub-markets have different levels of concern and sophistication (e.g. amongst occupiers, retailers tend to be more aware of the importance of design quality than office users).

■ **Poor information** about the preferences of prospective occupiers and investors, especially in the case of speculative developments. This adds to the risk of diverging from standards of design quality that are perceived to be 'safe'.

■ **The timing of a development** in relation to the ups and downs of the property and investment market will affect perceived risk and therefore attitudes towards investing in urban design quality.

- **Small and piecemeal development** is less likely to bring to the fore issues of 'place-making' and makes it harder for investors to capture externalities in the form of rents and capital values.

- **High land costs** can reduce profit margins and leave little room for investment in quality, especially since in property markets prices adjust only slowly and imperfectly.

- **Fragmented patterns of land ownership** can increase the time and the uncertainty of the development process and lead to fragmented design solutions.

- **Combative relationships** between developers and the public sector increase the time taken to develop and thus add to uncertainty and risk.

- **The economic environment**, which if dominated by high inflation and high interest rates (frequently the case in the UK since the 1960s) will lead to shorter term investment decisions and to less investment in design.

- **Lack of choice**. Constraints in the supply of the right quality of property in the right location can make good design less of a priority in occupier decision-making – if the right location does not have good quality space on offer, occupiers will opt for lower quality development rather than another location.

- **Short-term planning**. The structure of capital markets, with planning horizons of three to five years, makes it difficult for many businesses to engage in the long-term planning necessary for delivery of good design.

- **Perceptions of cost**. Occupiers perceive that, although many of the benefits of good design accrue to the wider community, it is they who will pay for it in the form of higher rent, running costs and commercial rates.

- **Decision-making patterns**. Many of the most important urban design decisions are taken not by planners, developers or designers but by people who may not think of themselves as being involved in urban design at all (e.g. quantity surveyors and accountants).

- **Reactionary approaches to urban design** across local authorities and a general failure to link urban regeneration and good urban design.

- **Low levels of urban design skills** on both sides of the development process.

For all stakeholders, constraints on investment in good design are not fixed in time. Property markets are cyclical and therefore the relationships between stakeholders change. In an 'occupier's market', occupiers' needs in terms of space quality dictate far more directly what is produced by developers and bought by investors. In a 'developer's market', occupiers have to take whatever is on offer. Nevertheless, it is not just the relative position of hierarchies of considerations that change over time. As the negotiating power of stakeholders shifts, there are also changes in who pays for what in terms of running costs and some of the design-related 'externalities' affecting a development (Guy, 1998).

Barriers to delivering better urban design are complex and require a range of solutions. Showing that good urban design adds value might, however, provide the necessary incentive to overcome many of the market, political and skills-based difficulties that together hold back a general improvement in urban design quality.

5.0 The Case Studies

5.1 An analytical framework

VARIOUS approaches to measuring the value of urban design were examined during the literature and research review. At one end of the spectrum lay qualitative assessments of the value of design based on stakeholders' perceptions of value in the context of their own motivations. At the other end were complex econometric exercises aiming towards a cost–benefit analysis of good design.

It was concluded that the best way of assessing value in urban design was through an eclectic 'common-sense' approach. This looked at how different stakeholders perceived the value – or the broadly defined costs and benefits – of urban design and compared it with quantitative indicators of success.

As was clear from previous attempts at assessing and measuring design value, quantitative and qualitative assessments of the costs and benefits of good design are closely interlinked. The measurable commercial success – or otherwise – of good design in the form of higher rents, turnover or capital values reflects how developers, investors, occupiers and the general public perceive the attractiveness of certain types of urban locations and developments. This interdependence could be used to inform the methodology.

The analytical framework was therefore based on a simplified version of the list of possible costs and values for urban design presented in Tables 3 and 4. In Table 8, these concerns are grouped into three dimensions reflecting the notion of overarching sustainable value. The first addresses the economic viability of urban design and is further distinguished between

■ the pure economic performance of investment in good design – including the costs and benefits that are usually measured in this kind of exercise (e.g. Vandell & Lane, 1989; Property Council of Australia, 1999)

■ the direct and indirect value associated with the operational performance of a development – such as the running costs and effects on occupiers' productivity and business performance

■ the costs associated with the production of good urban design

■ the wider impacts of good urban design, for example on area regeneration and the viability of the locality.

The second and third dimensions deal with the social and environmental benefits of good urban design.

Not all the costs and benefits of good urban design could be assessed within the scope of the project. Some represent the cumulative outcome of several episodes of good design or will only be visible over a long time. Others are perceived as benefits by stakeholders but are difficult to assess or quantify – a feeling of inclusiveness, for example. For some, there are clear quantifiable indicators of success, such as better financial returns on investment. For others, the criteria defining success are much less clear-cut but can nevertheless be appraised by qualitative means – the well-being of the workforce might come into this category. On this basis, a number of indicators were selected representing each of the three dimensions of value.

Table 8: Analytical Framework to Assess and Measure the Value of Good Urban Design

Dimensions of Value		Possible Indicators	Quantitative Assessment	Qualitative Assessment	Comments
Economic Viability	**Economic performance of investment in good urban design**	▪ Rental values ▪ Capital Values ▪ Vacancy rates ▪ Take-up rates ▪ Investment availability	▪ Comparison of rental values, capital values, vacancy rates and take-up rates of selected developments with average for similar types of property	▪ Interview questions to developers, investors and, occupiers, addressing their views on the economic performance of the development	▪ Average figures for rents and capital values from the Investment Property Databank (IPD) or local property firms ▪ Average figures for vacancy and take-up rates possibly from local property firms
	Operational performance of good urban design	▪ Management costs ▪ Security expenditure ▪ Energy consumption ▪ Accessibility ▪ Productivity of occupier ▪ Health and satisfaction of workforce ▪ Corporate imaging	▪ If available, data for individual developments on energy consumption, management costs, productivity, etc., which could be compared within cases or on a broader basis if information is available	▪ Interview questions to occupiers addressing the running costs of the development and the influence of urban design on their corporate performance	▪ Quantitative information might be possible for individual developments, but there are problems in finding comparators
	Production of good urban design	▪ Production costs ▪ Infrastructure costs ▪ Duration of planning approval process ▪ Prestige and reputation	▪ Comparison of production and infrastructure costs and duration of planning negotiation for the selected developments, within sample of cases and with average for similar types of property	▪ Interview questions to developers addressing production costs, the planning process, infrastructure costs, and the impact of the development on their standing in the marketplace ▪ Interview questions to local authority officials on infrastructure costs and the planning process	▪ Average figures for production costs from construction industry publications ▪ Average duration of planning process from local authorities
	Area regeneration/ viability impact of good urban design	▪ Local property values ▪ Place-marketing ▪ Area revitalisation	▪ Evolution of land and property values around the selected developments compared to the average in the locality	▪ Interview questions to local authority officials and local economic development partnerships on impact of development on the local economy	▪ Average figures for property values in surrounding area from local estate agents
Social Benefit		▪ Identity/civic pride ▪ Place vitality ▪ Inclusiveness ▪ Connectivity ▪ Safety ▪ Facilities and amenities	▪ If available, data on footfall for mixed use cases with retail, compared to average for locality (vitality)	▪ Interview questions to local authority officials and sample of local community addressing issues of place-identity, vitality and inclusiveness	▪ Quantitative information on vitality might be possible for individual developments, but difficulties with comparators
Environmental Support		▪ Energy consumption ▪ Accessibility ▪ Traffic generation ▪ Greenery/ecology	▪ If available, data for individual developments on energy consumption, modes of transport, traffic generation, commuting times, etc., for comparison between cases or on a broader basis	▪ Interview questions to occupiers, local authority officials and sample of local community addressing the environmental impacts of the development	▪ Average figures for energy consumption (and possibly traffic generation, modes of transport for users/occupiers) by type of development are available from specialised research institutions

5.2 Choosing the case studies

A case study approach was chosen as the only feasible means of gathering the necessary qualitative and quantitative data – particularly given the likely commercial sensitivity of some of that data. Selection of case studies therefore formed an important part of the research.

Funds enabled the selection of up to six in-depth case studies, a number equivalent to the RICS & DoE funded work but far fewer than either the Australian or American projects discussed in Section 4.7 (respectively these covered 16 and 102 developments, although analysis was limited to quantitative data). To allow meaningful conclusions to be drawn from a small number of case studies, developments were compared which were similar in all respects except their urban design. To this end the case studies were limited to commercial workplaces, and paired developments from the same regions and market contexts were chosen. Pairs were also chosen to exhibit a variety of practice in speculative commercial urban design. By these means it was effectively possible to discount, within the pairs, factors such as development use, location (broadly defined), occupier type, investor type and developer type.

Suitable pairs proved difficult to identify. The relative quality of practice was not always clear-cut and market contexts varied more than expected. Finally, however, three pairs were selected: one from the East Midlands – Castle Wharf and Standard Court in Nottingham – one from the West Midlands – Brindleyplace (Birmingham) and Waterfront (Dudley) – and one from the North West – Barbirolli Square (Manchester) and Exchange Quay (Salford). All were

■ commercial, predominantly office developments, but including other uses and containing significant areas of public/semi-public open space

■ built at roughly the same time.

For each case study development, an on-site urban design analysis was undertaken by the research team using the tool presented in Figure 2. The results of these analyses are included as Annex B. Interviews were then conducted, wherever possible in person, with representatives of the investor, developer and designer organisations; with the key planning officer(s); with an economic development officer (where one existed); with at least two occupier organisations; and with a range of everyday users of the public/semi-public spaces. At least ten interviews were conducted per case study.

Interviews sought quantitative data to back up the qualitative responses of interviewees and followed a structure based on the issues identified in Table 8. (The interview pro-formas for each category of interviewee are included as Annex C.) With the exception of everyday users, interviewees were given the opportunity to complete an urban design assessment of their own.

A review of the case studies follows, including a summary of the individual urban design assessments and of the quantitative evidence for each case study pair. The following section explores in depth the qualitative evidence on economic, social and environmental value, whilst in Section 7 conclusions are drawn from across the empirical research work.

5.3 Case Study Review

5.3.1 East Midlands (Castle Wharf, Nottingham, and Standard Court, Nottingham)

Nottingham is a strong service and business centre for the East Midlands region, with a particularly successful shopping centre which is relatively free from out-of-town competition. The city centre is bounded on the north and south by shopping precincts. The city's smallish stock of office space is distributed across the centre and its fringes, with the major addition of 400,000 square feet in the new Inland Revenue development south of the railway station. Castle Wharf adjoins a canal which lies between the city core and the station. Standard Court lies to the extreme west of the centre just north of Nottingham Castle.

Figure 3: Nottingham, Annual % Growth in Office Capital Values (source: derived from IPD data)

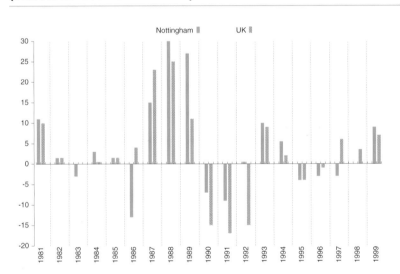

Figure 4: Nottingham Office Rental Returns (source: derived from IPD data)

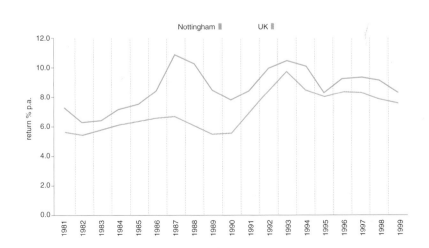

Nottingham experienced the 1980s office boom late and in acute form (see Figures 3 and 4), but subsequent falls in capital values and in rental returns to office investors were less severe than the national average, reflecting in part the relatively diverse local economy. Capital values of office investments in Nottingham have tended to settle at levels that give investors annual yields of 7–8%.

The city has for some time been concerned to offer high quality retail provision and an attractive urban environment and in recent years has extended that concern beyond the primary retail core. The City Planning Department has an active urban design team and various initiatives have been directed towards producing coherent advice on design quality. High-profile developments such as the Inland Revenue Headquarters and the Jubilee Campus at Nottingham University, both designed by Michael Hopkins and Partners, have helped to raise the profile of design within the city.

Castle Wharf, Nottingham

- **Areas:** Commercial space: approximately 15,000 m^2. Retail, restaurants: 10,500 m^2

- **Total Area of Site:** 1.3 ha

- **Usage:** Offices, retail and leisure

- **Owners:** Nottingham Evening Post (NEP building), Charles Street (BT and NatWest buildings), Greenalls, British Waterways

- **Occupiers:** Nottingham Evening Post as major occupier, BT, NatWest, several retail operators, restaurants and bars (also Magistrates' Court as part of the new area if not actually part of the development)

- **Development Finance:** Castle Wharf Developments, pre-sale scheme with Nottingham Evening Post

- **Developer:** First attempt by Norcross, then Castle Wharf Developments

- **Design:** Franklin Ellis

Background

Castle Wharf is a mixed-use scheme comprising offices, leisure and retail space and incorporating part of the Beeston Canal as it passes through Nottingham. The edge-of-centre site incorporates land that was originally owned by the local authority, by private owners and by British Waterways. Before redevelopment it contained several industrial buildings, warehouses, retail premises and a British Waterways depot. In the mid-1980s a masterplan was prepared for the site as part of an effort by the local authority to unlock development potential in canalside locations. A design brief followed in the early 1990s.

Figure 5: Castle Wharf Layout

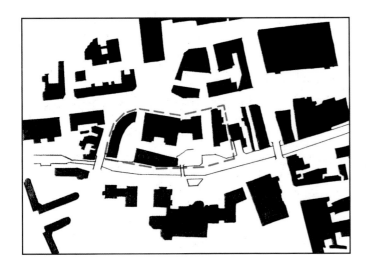

An attempt by developers Norcross to redevelop part of the site was unsuccessful, as was the first proposal by Castle Wharf Developments. After an informal design competition, Castle Wharf Developments submitted a revised scheme for a major office-based mixed-use development. Included in the negotiation for planning permission was the construction of a new bridge over the canal and the demolition of a number of locally listed buildings. Improving links between the site and the town centre and Inland Revenue development was also required. Planning permission was given in 1996.

The development received no grant aid, but once the Nottingham Evening Post agreed to take space the scheme became viable. As initially planned, the development provided a little over 9,000 m^2 of offices, mostly to accommodate the Nottingham Evening Post, but this was increased to nearly 15,000 m^2 after BT and NatWest expressed an interest in relocating to the area.

Construction was based on a design-and-build contract and was undertaken to a tight schedule. The development was completed in 1999 and is now sold entirely to investors. It has won a number of local awards.

Urban design

Castle Wharf received a research team rating of 29 out of 35 (equal highest of the case studies). The scheme helps to move the centre of gravity of Nottingham southwards, opening up a range of other sites along the city's south side. It builds on the long established industrial canal heritage of the area to create a distinct sense of place. Yet the environment is a contemporary one and a high quality public realm is complemented by the insertion of good commercial buildings (although the public ones are less architecturally successful).

Figure 6: Castle Wharf – a vibrant new public place mixing life giving activities with commercial uses

In a highly constrained site, the development starts to make connections back into the city, across and along the canal and to Nottingham's main railway station. It offers an environment that, with its broad range of work and leisure uses, is well used throughout the day and into the night. The key public spaces are well articulated, animated by the range of uses and are highly legible, offering good visual links with surrounding areas. They provide a safe, attractive and functional environment. Assessments of the urban design qualities of the scheme by the architect and occupiers largely supported that of the research team, rating the development 31 and 29 respectively, with current ease of movement cited as the major problem in the former assessment and adaptability in the latter.

Figure 7: Castle Wharf – a successful and permeable sequence of new public spaces positioned along the canal

Viability

At Castle Wharf two of the major occupiers – the Nottingham Evening Post and Greenalls – were effectively project partners and are now freehold owners of their space. Other occupiers, including BT and NatWest, came in later but still early enough to influence internal specification. They are now renting from the same investor.

The costs of design work and especially of infrastructure and building were high, more because of the local authority's conservation requirements than because of urban design demands. Thus high standards were achieved in finishes and hard landscaping, in layout, in resolving problems of connectivity to the surrounding areas and in the mix of uses. The location is now very popular, resulting in rising asset values for the owner-occupying firms. For the tenant firms this popularity is reflected in rents which are among the highest in Nottingham.

Prospects for continuing growth in the value of the scheme are good, partly because a plan to move the inner ring road will greatly improve the pedestrian environment and connections. The initial developers, however, seem to have missed the enhanced financial gains from their scheme, having sold their part interest to Charles Street at a price which gave them only about half the return (7–8%) that they might have expected. Good urban design – including in this instance a good strategy for the city core which generated the location – seems to have played a powerful role in giving Nottingham a new group of buildings with outstanding value in financial and broader terms.

Standard Court, Nottingham

- **Areas:** Office space approximately 8,300 m^2. Retail and leisure approximately 870 m^2. Residential units: 130 flats
- **Total Area of Site:** 2.6 ha
- **Usage:** Offices, restaurant facilities and housing
- **Occupiers:** Nottingham Health Authority, bar and restaurant operators (Harts), Eversheds, residents
- **Development Finance:** PFI-style operation involving the Health Authority, Norwich Union, and Mill Group
- **Developer:** Nottingham Health Authority (conception of overall scheme), Mill Group (developer on behalf of NUPPP)
- **Design:** Crampin and Pring

Background

Standard Court is a mixed-use development separated from the city centre by a major road – Maid Marion Way. It comprises office space, residential units and three retail/restaurant units. The trigger for the development was the closure of the hospital that occupied the site, with the initial scheme based on the re-use of a 1960s tower block (the Trent Wing extension of the hospital) as the Health Authority headquarters. However, the local authority required the demolition of the tower block as a condition of the redevelopment.

Figure 8: Standard Court Layout

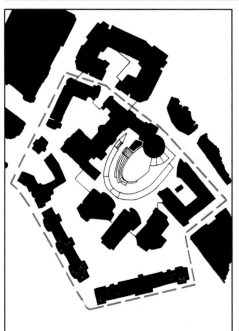

Nottingham Health Authority – the original owners of the site – did not by themselves have the resources to demolish the tower block and redevelop the site. On the advice of the design team, they sought PFI-style private sector funding and EU gap funding. The latter was granted on condition that the listed buildings would be renovated, the tower block demolished and a new public open space provided. The private partners were Norwich Union and the Mill Group, a property and finance company. Norwich Union were at the time looking for a pilot case through which they could develop an approach to further PFI involvement.

Outline planning permission was given in 1993 and detailed permissions over the following two years. The scheme started on site in 1996 and is now complete apart from some residential development.

Urban design

Standard Court has been less successful than Castle Wharf in revitalising its immediate environment. The new public arena remains largely unused and desolate, even on the sunniest days, and its physical fabric seems uncared for. On the plus side, contemporary and historic buildings are successfully integrated and one of the most intrusive tower blocks on the Nottingham skyline has been demolished.

Figure 9: Standard Court: The Arena – imposing, but desolate and disconnected

The overall impression is of a disconnected place that does not welcome people in and offers them little once they are there. The few active uses are tucked away or have not been let. The main entrances to the private office buildings

do not face onto the arena. In urban design terms this is clearly a missed opportunity, all the more so given the potential offered by an historic location next to Nottingham Castle. Significantly, the occupiers and investor largely concurred with the research team's urban design assessment of 14, rating the development 13 and 15 respectively.

Figure 10: Standard Court – a successful mixing of old and new

Viability

Standard Court is a strong contrast to Castle Wharf. Its core is office accommodation for the Regional Health Authority, on a site chosen not for its optimal attributes but because the Authority happened to own it. The cost of removing the Trent Wing left the development marginal throughout its planning stages.

Even though the site is not on a busy route, or indeed on the way to anywhere, it was decided to incorporate retail and catering premises. In the absence of passing trade, these could flourish only if they became destinations in themselves, which, the restaurant apart, has not yet happened. Other regenerative effects of the scheme have been limited and later development in the area has been largely residential.

From a financial point of view, the Health Authority seems content – though they attribute this more to the efficiency gain of being in a new building and to the money they made by selling off their other properties than to the economic advantages of Standard Court. In the tenanted part of the scheme, rents have been below the best Nottingham levels and the investors – Mill Group – consider the project to have been satisfactory but not excellent. No full capital valuation is available but the investor estimates the scheme to be worth about £3.7m. The main beneficiary seems to have been the investor, Norwich Union.

In short, the Health Authority has the premises it specified and wants while the investor has an assured short-term – and long-term – return understood to be starting at 8% per annum, above what might have been expected. The initial investor interest was indeed largely generated by the prospect of achieving a good long-term income stream.

5.3.2 West Midlands (Brindleyplace, Birmingham, and Waterfront Business Park, Dudley)

The West Midlands has experienced rapid and often painful loss of established industrial activity in recent decades, alongside very uneven growth in tertiary activities and new forms of manufacturing. In response, Birmingham City Centre has experienced major changes designed to raise its profile and attractiveness as a business, cultural and office location and as a shopping centre that can compete with suburban malls. The Birmingham case study focused on part of the central transformation, while the Dudley study examined a business park on a former steelworks site in the west of the region, adjacent to the Merry Hill shopping mall.

The office property market in the West Midlands (and Birmingham within it) experienced the boom of the late 1980s in dramatic form, as Figure 11 shows, although the fall in capital values in the early 1990s was less steep than for the UK as a whole. Thus in recent years the office market in Birmingham has been markedly more stable than the national average.

Figure 11: Birmingham & West Midlands: Annual % Growth in Office Capital Values (source: Investment Property Database)

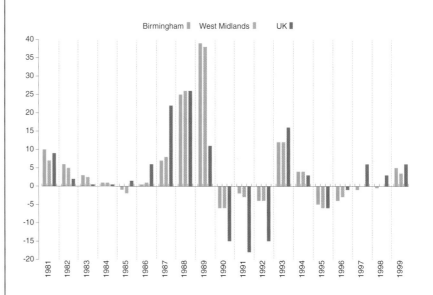

For over ten years, Birmingham City Council has been at the forefront of supporting good urban design and providing a positive policy and administrative structure through which to deliver it. Dudley Metropolitan Borough Council has not been so proactive, in part no doubt because of the different (less dynamic) market context found in the Black Country; and in any event the location of the Dudley case study within an Enterprise Zone tended to undermine any local authority concern for design that might have existed. Dudley MBC has since determined that urban design will need to play a much bigger role in promoting sustainable regeneration and has used the revision of the Unitary Development Plan to set in place a long-term urban design framework for the case study area.

Figure 12: Birmingham & West Midlands Office Rental Returns (source: Investment Property Database)

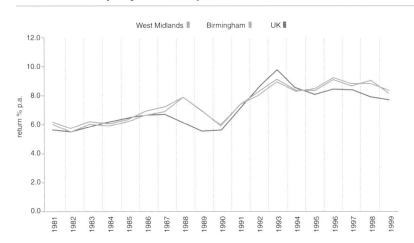

Brindleyplace, Birmingham

- **Areas:** Office space: 1.1 million ft^2 (approximately 102,300 m^2). Retail and restaurants: 170,000 ft^2 (approximately 15,740 m^2)

- **Total Area of Site:** 6.9 ha

- **Usage:** Offices, leisure, hotel, residential (in separate location within site), café/restaurant/bar, and retail units

- **Owners:** Birmingham City Council as freeholders and several leaseholders on long leases, chief among them Argent (undeveloped plots and completed office space), British Airways Pension Trustees (Water's Edge and No. 1), BT Pension Scheme (Nos 3, 4 and 5), Vardon (Sealife Centre), Citibank and UBK (Nos 3 and 4)

- **Occupiers:** BT (No. 5), Lloyds TSB (No. 2), other main buildings with multiple occupiers

- **Development Finance:** Argent Group Plc, orchestrating various investment packages for the different stages of the development, and involving among others BA Pension Trustees, Berkeley (now Crosby) Homes, Greenalls, the Institute of Electrical Engineers, Vardon, BT Pension Scheme, Citibank, UBK, Thames Valley Park, Governor's House

- **Developer:** Argent Group Plc

- **Design:** Terry Farrell/John Chatwin (main square, masterplan, infrastructure and Crescent Theatre), Townshend Landscape Architects (landscaping and Oozells Square), Benoy (Water's Edge and multi-storey car park), Levitt Bernstein (Oozells Street School refurbishment and Ikon Gallery), Anthony Peake Associates (No. 1), Allies & Morrison (Nos 2 and 6), Porphyrios Associates (Nos 3 and 7), Stanton Williams (No. 4), Sidell Gibson Partnership (Nos 5, 8 and 10), Associated Architects (No. 9), CZWG (Café), Hulme Upright Weedon (Hotel), Lyons Sleeman Hoare (Triangle Housing), Foster & Partners (National Sealife Centre), David Robotham (Institute of Electrical Engineers), John Dixon & Associates (Greenalls Pub)

Background

Brindleyplace is a mixed-use (mainly office-based) scheme in the centre of Birmingham which describes itself as one of Europe's largest inner city developments. In 1987, Birmingham City Council, seeking a private sector developer to build a scheme to complement the National Indoor Arena and International Convention Centre, invited tenders for the site. Merlin Shearwater Laing was selected and bought a 125 year lease for £23m. Outline planning permission was granted in 1988, with the Percy Thomas Partnership and Fitch Benoy as masterplanners. Shortly after, however, Laing bid successfully for the National Indoor Arena contract and pulled out of the consortium, leading to the formation of Brindleyplace plc, a joint venture company between Merlin and Shearwater (a subsidiary of Rosehaugh).

Figure 13: Brindleyplace Layout

Shearwater went into liquidation in 1990 and ownership of the site reverted to Rosehaugh with Terry Farrell as architect. In 1993, after Rosehaugh itself went into receivership, Argent purchased the site for £3m, with a revised 150 year lease. John Chatwin (a former partner of Terry Farrell) was appointed as masterplanner.

The first phase of the development – the Water's Edge – was entirely funded by Argent and built speculatively as part of the headlease obligation imposed by Birmingham City Council. In 1994, after some of the units at Water's Edge were let, the end investment was sold to the British Airways Pension fund trustees on the basis that they would forward-fund the speculative construction of No. 1 Brindleyplace.

Later phases included site sales to Berkeley Homes, Greenalls and the Institute of Electrical Engineers. These deals financed the construction of the central square and the main part of the infrastructure for the site. The latest phase to be completed includes Oozells Square and Nos 6 and 9 Brindleyplace. Most recently, there has been a site sale with development obligation for a hotel and progress has been made towards the development of Nos 8 and 10, both mixed-use buildings providing offices and residential accommodation. The development has won a range of local and national design awards.

Urban design

Brindleyplace shared with Castle Wharf the highest overall research team rating of 29, reflecting the high quality commercial environment that has been created. Developers have been able to create a new urban quarter around a network of well-defined and coherent new public spaces. The centre of gravity of the city has been extended across the inner ring road, offering considerable design benefits and linkages at a larger spatial scale.

Figure 14: Brindleyplace – a well enclosed, safe and attractive public realm

Today, Brindleyplace is enjoyed by a wide range of users who feel comfortable in the area and who are easily able to navigate through the simple grid masterplan. The development is, however, clearly privately owned and has a slightly exclusive, highly commercial character. The strong security guard presence reinforces this feeling. It is also to some degree a 'manufactured' environment, with the range of uses more clearly zoned into different parts of the site than would be the case in a traditional urban environment. Nevertheless, the range of uses and the mix of public and private activities ensure that the key spaces are animated throughout the day. It has also been possible to integrate a number of existing high quality buildings into the masterplan, and partly because of this the development relates well to its historic canalside setting. The developer and designer largely confirmed this assessment, giving Brindleyplace a slightly higher rating at 31 and 30 respectively, while recognising that some of its interfaces and linkages with the surrounding area have not been as successfully designed as they might have been and that at night some of the minor routes are not pedestrian-friendly.

Figure 15: Brindleyplace – successfully mixing uses in a highly legible sequence of spaces

Viability

Brindleyplace initially fell foul of the recession in the early 1990s. As a result, Argent plc was able to buy the 17 acre site from the receiver at the price – often described as 'low' – of £3m. This helped Argent to cover decontamination costs of £0.5m, marketing costs above £3m and infrastructure spending of about £12m and to deliver a good quality of urban design. (The developer estimates a high design cost of 11% of total investment.)

In its edge-of-centre location, Brindleyplace is in competition with the city core (where public transport access is good and much business can be done on foot) and with other off-centre developments, especially the Blythe Valley Business Park which has twice as many parking spaces per worker. Although rents for offices and restaurants have at least doubled since the start of the scheme, reaching a peak of £25 per square foot in 1996, they have since fallen back to about £22, in line with regional trends.

Significant parts of the scheme are unlet, but construction of the later phases continues apace. The average yield figure of 6.5% gives grounds for optimism. Furthermore, a Metro Line is expected to serve the area within two years which will reduce the access problems and boost rents and values. Significantly, the housing element of the scheme, accepted in the first instance rather reluctantly by the developer, was expected to sell at about £75 per square foot but is now changing hands at two to three times that price. The developer now considers that with hindsight more housing might usefully have been included.

In terms of wider economic impact, Brindleyplace is viewed very positively. It has been a powerful catalyst for further development in adjoining parts of Birmingham, has created a popular new open space for the city and has created jobs.

Waterfront Business Park, Dudley

- **Areas:** 190,000 ft^2 (approximately 17,600 m^2). Retail and restaurants: 170,000 ft^2 (approximately 15,740 m^2)
- **Total Area of Site:** 6.96 ha
- **Usage:** Offices, leisure, hotel (the only four star hotel in the Black Country) and business sheds with approximately 2000 car parking spaces
- **Owners:** Chelsfield plc owns most of the development, most of the adjoining land and Merry Hill Shopping Centre. A few buildings are owned by their occupiers, including the dominant Point North building (Prudential)
- **Occupiers:** Many of the buildings are in multiple occupancy with the exception of the large sheds, the Point North building (Prudential), the hotel (Copthorne). Several public sector agencies and quangos are now occupiers (Inland Revenue, TEC, etc.)
- **Development Finance:** Initially Richardson Developments, banks; later Chelsfield plc
- **Developer:** Richardson Developments Ltd
- **Design:** Level 7 Architects, Building Design Partnership

Background

Situated to the west of Birmingham, near Brierley Hill town centre, the Waterfront Business Park incorporates a mix of business, retail and leisure uses. The site originally housed one of the biggest steelworks in the country. Following its closure in 1982, the 97 acre site remained empty for several years.

Figure 16: Waterfront Business Park Layout

In 1984, Dudley Enterprise Zone was extended to encompass the site and it was developed in two stages by Richardson Developments – first into the Merry Hill Shopping Centre, which initially met with local opposition, and later into the Waterfront Business Park which commenced in 1990. The development was bought by its current owners, Chelsfield plc, in 1998.

The Dudley Canal forms the heart of the development, surrounded by leisure uses including pubs, bars, restaurants, nightclubs, the region's first four star hotel and a fitness centre. During the day the development mainly attracts those working in the area, but at night it acts as a magnet for young people in the nearby towns of Brierley Hill, Dudley and Kidderminster.

The scheme is not yet complete, with further development being planned on the car park on the eastern side. Dudley MBC, in conjunction with Chelsfield plc, have prepared a comprehensive strategy for the area with the aim of creating a new town centre within the Brierley Hill/Merry Hill/Waterfront triangle. A new branch of the Metro Line is planned and remedial action is proposed on the urban design front.

Urban design

Waterfront was built at around the same time as Brindleyplace but in urban design terms is very different. Essentially, the development provides a formula business park environment on a brownfield site – a type not renowned for urban design quality, tending as it does to be dominated by roads and parking. Waterfront suffers from just these problems, particularly around its periphery and in its later phases. Nevertheless, a serious attempt has been made to inject a sense of place through high quality soft landscaping, a formal layout and by relating the development to the canal. It has also created a vibrant oasis through its range of popular bars and restaurants in the middle of what was a bleak former industrial landscape.

Figure 17: Waterfront – in parts a car-dominated formula business park

That said, the scheme lacks many key urban design qualities, not least proper connections with its immediate hinterland. Thus users need to rely heavily on private cars both to reach the development and to move around within it. Furthermore, although the development uses the canal as a focal point, much of the development suffers from a repetitive and non-contextual architectural idiom. The urban structure provided by the formal layout and relation to the canal breaks down quickly (as do the development's permeability and legibility) on moving away from the central axis. The research team gave the development a rating of 15, whilst the developer and investor both rated it 25. Interestingly, these stakeholders identified many of the same deficiencies as the research team, but perceived that the overall achievement of developing the site at all, and the qualities that had been secured in an otherwise hostile environment, outweighed the shortcomings.

Figure 18: Waterfront – in parts a highly successful and popular oasis in an otherwise bleak environment

Viability

The specification for the buildings and landscape at Waterfront was higher than the generally prevailing level for the region at the time, and rents were above the norm. This deterred some tenants. But the scheme has let well and rents are reported to have continued to rise in recent years, standing now at levels close to those in central Birmingham. This suggests that occupiers value the package they are getting – prestige buildings with generous car parking and recreational facilities that appeal to staff. This combination of features – with urban design playing a part – has enabled the scheme to prosper despite some major drawbacks, including the acute inadequacy of the road and public transport infrastructure and the failure to relate the scheme to the nearby shopping centre or to Brierley Hill town centre. A monorail intended to compensate for some of these dislocations quickly failed.

Chelsfield plc note that rents of £12 per square foot are now being achieved for offices, with some occupiers paying more. The latest yield figure is 7.5% for an office let to a government client on a 15 year institutional lease. This strong financial performance reflects the fact that the scheme was the first business park in the region, has since lacked nearby alternatives and has good prospects for further expansion, infrastructure improvements and remedial urban design work.

Having attracted about 4,000 jobs and a new class of customers for its leisure activities, the project has also made a strong contribution to economic growth and regeneration in the sub-region.

5.3.3 North West (Barbirolli Square, Manchester, and Exchange Quay, Salford)

The economy of Manchester has undergone a rapid restructuring in the last two decades, losing much of its manufacturing and port-related activity and replacing it with a growing tertiary sector – business services, retail, cultural and educational activities, many associated with new or transformed venues and a dramatically redesigned city centre. Barbirolli Square is a transformed site on the western edge of the centre, whilst Exchange Quay was an early development within the Enterprise Zone designated in nearby Salford. Both developments are served by the Metro system.

Figure 19: Manchester and Salford: Annual % Growth in Office Capital Values (source: IPD)

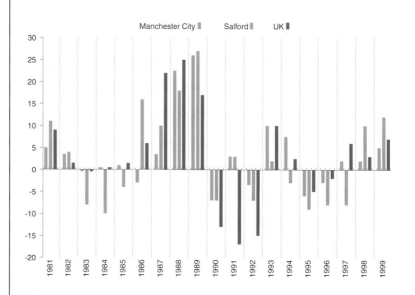

Figure 20: Manchester and Salford Office Rental Returns (source: IPD)

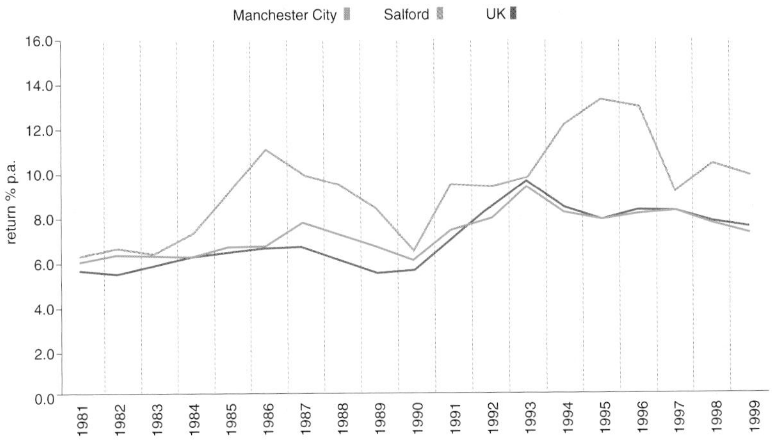

In recent years, local authorities in both Manchester and Salford have given a higher priority to urban design. In Manchester, the experience of successfully redeveloping both the Hulme housing estate in the south of the city and the city centre itself (following a terrorist bomb) has led to a renaissance in urban design.

In Salford, the closure of the docks and associated industry encouraged the planning authority to develop a new urban design framework for Salford Quays. The new infrastructure is now beginning to pay dividends, not least in bringing to Salford the new Lowry Centre. Significantly, the Salford case study fell outside the framework area and relates poorly to it, being part of the earlier Enterprise Zone with its associated laissez-faire approach to urban design.

Barbirolli Square, Manchester

- **Areas:** Commercial space: 22,000 m² offices. Retail and restaurants: 800 m². Bridgewater Hall (2,400 seats)

- **Total Area of Site:** 1 ha

- **Usage:** Leisure and offices including a concert hall

- **Owners:** Hermes (offices), Hallé Concert Society (Bridgewater Hall)

- **Occupiers:** Multiple office users, mostly law firms and accountants (e.g. Masons, Addleshaw & Booths, Ernst & Young, Dibb Lupton Alsop), The Hallé Orchestra (Bridgewater Hall)

- **Development Finance:** Central Manchester Development Corporation, European Regional Development Fund, Hermes (offices)

- **Developer:** AMEC (offices), Beazer & Laing North West (Bridgewater Hall)

- **Design:** RHWL – initially just for the canal basin and the concert hall, but later commissioned by AMEC to design the office blocks as well

Background

The development comprises a free-standing concert hall (the Bridgewater Hall), two office blocks and a café/bar and represents one of a number of development initiatives west of Manchester City Centre. The area used to be part of the city's main public transport interchange with the Central Station. When the bus station closed, the site was earmarked for redevelopment in the local plan and later in the UDP.

Figure 21: Barbirolli Square Layout

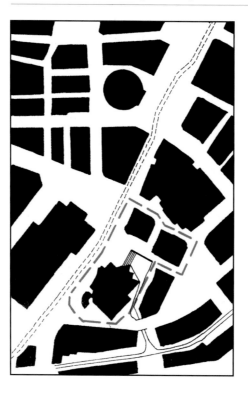

In 1988, the station site (by now compulsorily purchased by the local authority) was identified as a suitable home for the Hallé Orchestra, on condition that there should be some commercial development to help the regeneration process and the reintegration of the area into the city centre.

In 1990, the 'Bridgewater Initiative' was launched as a developer/architect competition (won by Beazer and RHWL) to design a new concert hall and develop the canal basin. Planning permission was obtained in 1992 and Government and European funding was in place by 1993. At the same time, the recession brought a serious property slump. This prompted a decision to use a design and build contract for the concert hall, with the mostly pre-let office development being built later under a different contract. The Barbirolli Square development was completed in the late 1990s and has since won awards from the Civic Trust and the RIBA.

Urban design

Barbirolli Square was one of the smallest of the developments examined, comprising two office blocks on one side of a square faced by the new Bridgewater Hall on the other. Nevertheless, the clever use of levels allows the central space to step down to a re-established canal basin onto which a new café opens up. The result is a gently animated public space with its own distinct character and sense of place and with a good quality of enclosure, despite the exposed position of the site next to a major road and tramway. The development also manages to respond well to existing high quality buildings and provides an attractive, legible and truly 'public' environment.

Figure 22: Barbirolli Square – a distinct new contemporary environment utilising the canal and change of levels to give a sense of place

The development knits this once derelict site back into the urban fabric and creates a new landmark gateway to Manchester. However, although good connections have been established on two sides of the new space, connectivity both across the main road and from the lower level space to the existing buildings opposite are compromised. Furthermore, the 'corporate style' office buildings and the introspective nature of the offices and Bridgewater Hall leave the higher levels devoid of active frontage, whilst parts of the hard landscaping are weathering poorly. These difficulties in detailed realisation

prompted a research team rating of 23. This assessment was broadly supported by the occupiers and investors, although not by the developer, who rated the development more highly at 30 but also acknowledged the limitations on pedestrian movement in and around the development.

Figure 23: Barbirolli Square – mixing old with new around a successful, if not always well connected, public space

Viability

The Bridgewater Hall was financed partly from the sale of the site for office development and partly from European funds. However, the original developer (Beazer), brought on board in the early 1990s, withdrew in the light of the worsening economic prospects for office development and a new agreement was reached with AMEC. Economic conditions in the mid-1990s were still not bright, and the single office block proposed at that time represented an uncomfortably large commitment. Investors finally signed up when the office scheme was split into two blocks, while the high quality of the urban design and the imposing setting helped to inspire confidence that the development would command prestige occupiers at premium rents.

The history of the development has so far fulfilled the ambitions of the developers, letting well (principally to law firms) and commanding the highest rents in Manchester. Most of the space was pre-let early on, allowing the occupiers to influence the detailed internal design of the development. Close co-operation between the public authorities, the developers and the architects meant that the formal approval process was also quick.

The office project cost £27.5m (including £0.2m funding for nearby Chepstow Square) and is now valued at £60m. The investors had, however, hoped for above-market returns in three years and were disappointed not to achieve them, although the high capital value suggests that further growth is expected.

Barbirolli Square pushes good design into an area where it was previously lacking. Its effect – conjoint with other developments on adjacent sites and around the GMex Centre – ripples out to produce cumulative economic growth. This is already visible in the five new restaurants that have opened in the surrounding area, while the development can be expected to push property values up faster in this district than in the city as a whole. Given the associated regeneration in the area and its increasing desirability, investors are likely to be happier when rent reviews begin than they have been in the first year or two.

Exchange Quay, Salford

- **Areas:** Office space: 1.1 million ft^2 (approximately 102,300 m^2). Retail and restaurants: 170,000 ft^2 (approximately 15,740 m^2)
- **Total Area of Site:** 3.04 ha
- **Usage:** Offices and small retail
- **Owners:** Master Trust, with 2300 different shareholders
- **Occupiers:** Multiple and single occupancy buildings accommodating 85 different tenants, among them insurance companies, banks, law firms and IT firms
- **Development Finance:** syndication involving several investors
- **Developer and Managers:** Initially Charter, then the Trust of investors, and after them Property Logistics, CIM and more recently Esterre Property Management (a subsidiary of Property Logistics)
- **Design:** Shepheard Gilmore/Shepheard Design

Background

Exchange Quay is situated on the banks of the Manchester Ship Canal/River Irwell at the southernmost point of Salford Quays, on the site of the old Manchester Docks and within the former Trafford Park Enterprise Zone. It was completed in 1991 and is mainly an office development, with a limited range of shops and restaurants intended for office workers.

Figure 24: Exchange Quay Layout

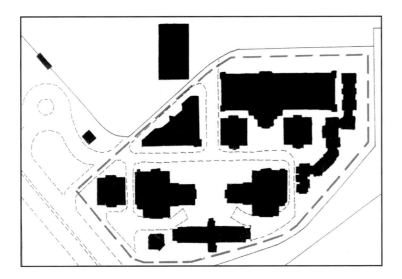

Exchange Quay was conceived during the boom period of the late 1980s as a type of office centre new to Manchester; a piece of Dallas which would attract large international corporate occupiers to a pioneering luxury enclave in a degraded dockside area. Investor confidence was booming in the North West until 1990 and the initial investment of about £200m was subscribed readily by a large number of international investors. Letting, however, proved a severe problem because by then demand nationally and regionally was in strong decline, with rents falling (see Figure 20). Instead of large corporate occupiers, only smaller users could be found and the offices had to be modified to fit multiple lettings.

In access terms, Exchange Quay now has its own Metrolink Station offering quick and easy access from Manchester City Centre. However, for the first eight years of its life the development was accessible only by car. The road network has since been improved with the construction of the City Link Expressway and the Trafford Road Bridge and dual carriageway, providing direct links to Manchester and the motorway network.

Urban design

Exchange Quay was rated lowest of the case studies by the research team, but much more highly by its own developer/investor – on a par with Brindleyplace and Castle Wharf. In part, the latter rating probably reflects the developer's current role as project estate manager and sales agent. Nevertheless, it shows how different stakeholders can make very different judgements on quality when seeing design issues from different perspectives (see Section

4.6). In comparison with the other case studies, the development is disconnected, turns its back on its surroundings and provides an internalised and largely car-dependent work environment. This feeling of introspection is compounded by the heavy security presence and by the high fences which surround the site and run between the office blocks and the waterfront. Many of these are, however, positive features from the Estate Manager's perspective.

Figure 25: Exchange Quay – the commercial heart of the scheme, a resting place

Internally, the development is laid out along a formal axis with some soft landscaping and 'public' art to soften the impact of the immense volume of building. One key space forms a central gathering point including a café and a number of retail units. The microclimate is poor (there is for example a wind tunnel effect) and the amenities are minimal, with the development overwhelmingly dominated by office uses and associated car parking. The buildings themselves are international in style, while the development almost completely turns its back on the Manchester Ship Canal next to the site. Any assessment of the urban design qualities of the scheme must, of course, be made in the knowledge that when conceived, the development sat in the middle of dereliction and decay and that any development at all was considered a triumph.

Figure 26: Exchange Quay – the approach to the scheme, high density, corporate and international in image

Viability

Today, the supply of offices in the Greater Manchester suburbs and region remains plentiful, so although demand for space in the development has recovered during the late 1990s, rents at Exchange Quay remain below or around the regional average. As a consequence, the original intention to give a return on investment over three to five years proved unrealistic. Returns remain low at 1–3% per annum, although investors are in the main retaining their shares in the hope of long-term profits. The development is almost fully let, and the investor/managers believe that the 'Dallas' style of urban and building design is a feature which – together with the adequate car parking – will make the scheme enduringly popular.

The initial investment cost was high, reflecting the high quality finishes and materials used between and in the buildings and the inflation of construction prices in the late 1980s boom (although these costs were offset to some extent by the simplicity of gaining permission in the Enterprise Zone and by the absence of planning obligations – only recently was a £2m contribution made to the Metro). Since completion, the project has benefited from high levels of care, maintenance and security. Because of the high density of the development and the comparative lack of common open space, service provision is concentrated in a small area. Costs are passed directly onto occupiers as service charges.

Beyond its internal financial history, the significant economic impacts of Exchange Quay appear to be just two – on traffic generation and on employment (there are now 4–5,000 people working on the site). There is little evidence of broader local economic impacts: retailers appear not to serve people from surrounding areas and people who work there appear to make little use of adjoining services.

6.0 The Stakeholders

6.1 The qualitative evidence

THE following discussion presents the views of each main stakeholder group on the economic, social and environmental value of good urban design.

Their views are important because only if key stakeholders sign up to the importance of good urban design can a shift in general (as opposed to exceptional) practice be expected to occur. What follows shows that changes in attitude have occurred, even if they are as yet far from universal. It is also clear that a number of the key barriers to the delivery of good urban design discussed above (see Section 4.10) are beginning to be overcome, particularly the piecemeal nature of much development, the lack of proactive approaches in public decision-making and the failure to link good urban design with value for money.

6.2 Investors' perspectives

Investors' perspectives on economic value

Investors' principal concern was to secure investments which provided

■ above market average incomes

■ potential for long-term income streams and/or capital growth

■ good quality covenants

■ buildings that have been well constructed or refurbished and, in some cases, open up new market potential.

Most investors also viewed urban design as an important factor in increasing sales and rental values. Along with issues such as access, parking, security, servicing (particularly for IT) and internal environmental control, environmental quality was seen as a key factor in occupier decision-making. The investor at Waterfront recognised that the deficit of urban design input in the original development needed to be rectified if the investment was to generate higher returns and further development opportunities in the future (hence their strong support for the designation of the area as an emerging town centre in the Unitary Development Plan (UDP)).

At Castle Wharf, the Nottingham Evening Post, which now owns and occupies a large part of the development, considered access and avoidance of disruption to employees' travel to work patterns to be the most important factors in their decision to invest. But they also wished their location to reflect the 'future spirit' of the city – that is, a mixed use area with facilities and amenities close at hand.

Significantly, Standard Court had been rejected as an alternative location for the Evening Post, in part because of its location but also because of the absence of 'life giving' elements. The key investors at Standard Court confirmed the development was having difficulty maintaining its mix of uses, with the bar struggling and the restaurant often quiet despite its good reputation. A small retail outlet facing onto the arena had never been let.

Exchange Quay had faced similar problems in its early years, although there the mid-1990s property slump was the main cause. Vacancy rates had initially been high and only through heavily discounted rents in its early years had occupancy improved to near 95%. Waterfront also suffered initial vacancy problems although more recently it has been achieving occupancy rates of 96%. Standard Court benefited from having a major client already on site and involved in promoting the development, but soon found that a lack of demand for offices required a change in the latter phases of the development towards high quality residential accommodation. By contrast, Barbirolli Square was 70% pre-let prior to completion and 100% let within a year of opening.

Along with location, investors considered urban design a factor in raising a development's profile. Castle Wharf, for example, offered the Evening Post the right kind of exposure, while the investor at Waterfront was concerned that some parts of the development needed upgrading to maintain prestige in what was the only development of its kind in the sub-region. All investors recognised that revitalisation of the areas around their developments had been achieved and land values increased, although in Salford and Dudley this was from a very low base and regeneration benefits had been much slower to ripple though the local economy than at Castle Wharf, Barbirolli Square and Brindleyplace.

Investors at Exchange Quay and Waterfront believed that distinct images for their developments had been achieved, albeit in the form of carefully controlled and secured environments. At Waterfront, the investor's long-term aspiration is now to reverse this isolation.

At Standard Court, the estate had been broken up into smaller and more manageable lots. The net result was a failure to consider the public parts of the site, which are now less easy to manage. Responsibility – and therefore the costs – are no longer spread across the estate but loaded onto one part. This has been a particular problem because maintenance was not fully considered during the design process and adds a further burden on the major investor, who commented that they would dearly like to be able to build over the new public arena. The inevitable result is a squeeze on maintenance standards. Investors at Castle Wharf reported that the high quality architectural and urban design of the development had allowed them significantly to reduce security, management and energy costs.

Investors' perspectives on social and environmental value

Investors generally felt that their developments provided clear social value through their regenerative impact and associated job creation. However, views about the social impact of the different design solutions were less clear. Most investors felt that their developments were attractive in themselves and generally responded well in design terms to their surroundings, although integration was not always an explicit objective. At Barbirolli Square, the architecture was described as deliberately very "Ally McBeal", a little piece of America in the middle of Manchester to present a strong corporate image. This, it was suggested, was highly valued by local politicians, who looked on the development with considerable pride as the first of its type in the city. The owner/investor at Castle Wharf similarly suggested that the development explicitly demonstrated how Nottingham was moving forward.

Investors at Exchange Quay, Castle Wharf and Waterfront all believed that they had created lively and vibrant places. At Standard Court, the investor felt that an opportunity had been missed, with the arena at the heart of the development doomed to failure because of the requirements of surrounding households and office users for a quiet environment, but also because of the absence of public conveniences on site, which made special events difficult to manage. The square was regarded as 'the wrong square in the wrong place' and therefore as a dead weight around the neck of the investor.

Whereas most investors felt their developments had a broader public role, at Exchange Quay the message was that

- people were only welcome if they had specific business there (the research team, for example, were stopped three times on the first visit and needed to get special permission to walk around and take photos)

- connectivity was an issue of guarding the edges of the development rather than one of integration

- only facilities and amenities necessary for the business activities of occupiers were appropriate on the site.

In other developments, the private nature of the 'public' spaces was often deliberately apparent (security guards in Brindleyplace, CCTV in Barbirolli Square and clear signage to maintain property rights at Standard Court). But with one exception (skateboarders at Standard Court) attempts at exclusion were not practised. Higher rated developments such as Castle Wharf had been designed with unobtrusive security and self-policing in mind and investors were generally pleased with the results.

All investors believed that their developments had had a positive impact on the local environment, mainly through bringing otherwise underused and derelict sites back into use. However, only the investor at Barbirolli Square had a corporate culture that routinely considered environmental factors in investment decisions. The company had introduced a sustainability policy and now considered issues such as reducing energy consumption, using higher quality materials and building higher quality public spaces (although not planting and ecology) as issues that positively influenced long-term investment returns. The company had concluded that such considerations were becoming more and more important, but that as yet only blue chip companies (which they aspired to attract to their developments) could afford such principles.

For all investors, key factors influencing economic value included parking and internal environment control, and although it was recognised that these factors had a serious environmental cost it was felt that market realities required their adequate provision. At Waterfront and Exchange Quay, for example, traffic generation was acknowledged to be a major (if unavoidable) problem. At Exchange Quay, an initial under-provision of parking had held back the letting of space. At Castle Wharf, investors were critical of the planning authority for deliberately restricting parking provision, although this had not affected the final decision to invest. Ecology was never regarded as a significant concern by investors because of the urban character of the locations. Nevertheless, the quality of planting was seen as an important concern in the more campus-like Exchange Quay and Waterfront developments.

6.3 Developers' perspectives

Developers' perspectives on economic value

For each of the developers design was important, although in different ways. The developers at Brindleyplace, Barbirolli Square and Castle Wharf took an urban, contextual approach to design, reacting in part to existing design briefs from planning departments. At Standard Court a similar approach was taken but without the benefit of a design brief. At Waterfront and Exchange Quay a more commercial approach was followed, with little or no early public sector involvement.

In Barbirolli Square, the challenge was to create a coherent urban design solution on a challenging and sloping site whilst reacting to the local authority's requirements for a space that was easy and cost effective to maintain, yet also secure and inviting. At Exchange Quay, the developers modelled the approach on Harbour Exchange in London Docklands as they sought to create a North American style, corporate, self-contained environment. In each development, therefore, design was important, but the relative balance between contextual concerns and commercial concerns determined the final design outcome.

The initial motivations of developers were primarily commercial. At Brindleyplace, the purchase of the site at a competitive price enabled the developers to move their company onto a larger stage and therefore in a new direction. At Waterfront and Exchange Quay, local developers recognised and took advantage of the opportunities provided by the designation of Enterprise Zones in both Dudley and Salford. Both were viewed as risky investments given the lack of previous commercial development in these areas, but in Dudley the developers were spurred on by a concern to help a local population hit by retrenchment in the steel industry. In Nottingham, the opportunity offered by the move of the Nottingham Evening Post provided the impetus to assemble and promote the Castle Wharf site.

All developers believed that the prestige attached to their developments was high. At Brindleyplace, Barbirolli Square and Castle Wharf, prestige was confirmed in the developers' minds by extensive coverage of their projects in the marketing literature for the city as a whole. These developers and the developer at Waterfront routinely used their schemes to market their own companies.

To the developers, the impact of the urban design solutions was decisive on a number of fronts, although location was considered the most important factor – for example, the developer at Brindleyplace was concerned that the location of the development – a 15 minute walk from the station – and the low city centre parking standards had lost potential tenants to nearby out of town developments. The developers at Waterfront were clear that the design and waterside setting of the development had contributed to achieving higher rental returns, although also to losing some potential tenants who were not prepared to pay for these benefits. At both Castle Wharf and Barbirolli Square, developers had been able to pre-let the schemes to high quality tenants on the basis of design (and location). Thus at Barbirolli Square, the tenants were sold the concept and subsequently took part in its detailed realisation. At Castle Wharf, tenants were also involved in the realisation and in achieving the higher office provision on the site. Although this provision went against the original local authority design brief that envisaged the retention of more existing buildings of townscape merit, it was achieved because of the high quality of the architectural and urban design solution proposed. In that sense, the tenant's requirements and the opportunities derived from good urban design delivered more lettable area.

Most developers either had difficulty attracting investors (Brindleyplace and Barbirolli Square) or largely financed their developments themselves (Castle Wharf, Standard Court and Waterfront). Nevertheless, following the development of Castle Wharf and the early phases of Brindleyplace, their developers were able to sell off sections to a range of investors. The perception was that the high quality achieved aided this process.

None of the developers felt that the planning process had been too long, with most commenting that the initial permission was achieved quickly as authorities did not want to forfeit regeneration opportunities. At Castle Wharf, however, detailed conservation and planning requirements had lengthened the design time and raised construction costs. Here, the developer commented that these costs were later recouped, but the process had been long and frustrating, and in his view and that of the marketing agent had not improved the end product.

Developers were all convinced that their developments had led to further regeneration in their respective areas, bringing jobs (some of which were new) and raising property prices. At Brindleyplace, for example, the site now includes hundreds of non-office jobs and has provided a model regeneration approach for the city, being reflected in more recent developments such as the Birmingham Mailbox. At Castle Wharf, the project had helped attract Capital One and the BBC to adjacent sites, continuing the regeneration of the south side of the city. The design quality achieved at Castle Wharf was perceived to be changing perceptions of that part of the city. The area around Barbirolli Square was regenerating from one with a rough reputation to one seen as the most prestigious office address in Manchester. At Standard Court the regenerative effects have been slower.

Developers' perspectives on social and environmental value

Developers were bullish about the social contribution their developments had made, arguing that their schemes were attractive, strengthened civic pride, enhanced social well-being (through improving the environment and providing jobs) and increased vitality (with the exception of Standard Court). On the related issues of providing facilities and amenities for the wider populace and encouraging an inclusive environment, there was less agreement. At Brindleyplace, Waterfront, Castle Wharf and Barbirolli Square all were welcome and vitality had been a key aim (in the case of Castle Wharf an explicit objective of the design competition organised by the developer). At Barbirolli Square the level of activity far exceeded expectations, extending well into the evening on the back of events in the concert hall. At Exchange Quay the approach was deliberately exclusive, with levels of activity driven by work patterns.

A similar division was apparent on issues of connectivity and integration. While integration was generally considered important by all developers, it had not been regarded as an early priority by the developers at Waterfront and Exchange Quay, who admitted that these concerns were being addressed retrospectively by investors and public authorities. Connectivity within and beyond the case study developments was also accepted as a weakness; at Castle Wharf it was argued that true integration would be feasible only once the Inner Ring Road had been moved (something outside the control of the developer), although efforts had been made to connect across the canal and enhance east/west linkages.

For developers, the regenerative impact of their projects flowed through to improvements in the local environment. However, only the developer at Barbirolli Square claimed that environmental issues had been important to them as a company; and only they and the developer at Castle Wharf suggested it was important to their clients (in the latter case only to BT, not to other occupiers on the site). Nevertheless, even there, the concept seemed limited to energy consumption within buildings and not to broader concerns for ecology or traffic generation. All developers accepted that the market imperative to maximise car parking remained, with the associated traffic generation problems seen as a fact of life. For schemes close to city centres, a lack of car parking was even seen as a competitive disadvantage, despite the acceptance that integration with the public transport network represented a bonus for occupiers.

Only the Barbirolli Square and Brindleyplace developers had initiated environmental BREEAM ratings for their buildings, although the Prudential building at Waterfront and BT building at Castle Wharf had ratings initiated by their occupiers. Significantly, the buildings at Brindleyplace were intended to be much more energy efficient but the developers concluded that clients would not be prepared to pay the extra up-front costs. At Barbirolli Square, where the development was aimed from the outset at the top end of the market, energy efficiency (including the provision of low-emissivity glass and bicycle storage) was deemed to be a sales point.

6.4 Designers' perspectives

Designers' perspectives on economic value

Designers viewed their role as balancing the commercial requirements of their clients with meeting the design expectations of the local authority. Inevitably, they argued, this involved compromises, with the success of the urban design solution dependent on the balance finally struck. Significantly, although all designers argued that urban design was fundamental to realising their developments, most were convinced that they could have done better. Nevertheless, all sites were deemed prestigious, with, for example, designers claiming that Brindleyplace had largely set the tone for regeneration across Birmingham while Waterfront provided a vibrant environment where none had existed before.

For the more successful urban design solutions in each pair, achieving high quality urban design was a key aspiration from the start. At Brindleyplace, for example, the urban design structure for the development had been defined early on by the local authority design framework. The designer's role was then seen as getting the best from the site in commercial terms whilst defining a coherent urban place. In this role much time was spent defending the level of public space provision against commercial pressures. At Castle Wharf, the designers undertook an initial feasibility study for the developer and later won a design competition. Their clear objective was to design the best urban space in Nottingham. At Barbirolli Square, the designers consciously used urban design to achieve coherence across the site, which was being developed under three separate contracts.

For the less successful urban design solutions, the designers observed that the difficulties and risks in making the developments happen to a large extent determined their final form. At Waterfront, the introspection of the development was dictated by the short-term uncertainties of making it viable in a difficult physical and commercial context. At Standard Court, the architect depended on the client's (limited) willingness to pay for good urban design. At Exchange Quay the design solution was not site-specific but imported from London Docklands.

Designers also reported that management costs were not on the whole a great concern to developers, who were chiefly concerned with capital costs and with meeting the requirements of their target tenant group. Thus large floorplates were the trend at the start of the design process for Brindleyplace and were thereafter a key factor in determining plot sizes and the block structure of the development. At Waterfront, the design concept, quality and specification had to deliver offices to the market at a competitive rate.

Designers' perspectives on social and environmental value

Designers saw an important role for their schemes in adding social value through site regeneration, the benefits of which they felt would trickle through to local populations, enhancing social well-being and civic pride. In some cases this impact was believed to be dramatic, for example at Waterfront because of the depressed economic and social position of the area. In such places, integration, access and connectivity had not been seen as early design priorities, whereas they had been at Standard Court because of the sensitive conservation context. At Brindleyplace, integration was deemed to have been successful because the development had not been designed by one architectural practice, whereas at Standard Court the application of a single hand was argued to have delivered better contextual integration.

Even where access and connectivity were a major concern, none of the designers believed they had achieved the optimum solution. At Brindleyplace, the site had originally been viewed as cut off and isolated by the canals and although it was now far better integrated, the designer argued it would still benefit from additional canal crossings (something the original budget forecasts did not stretch to). At Barbirolli Square, connectivity was considered good at the higher level, although the anxieties of occupiers in existing buildings had frustrated attempts to connect the development at lower levels. The designer at Standard Court did not consider the lack of connectivity to be a problem.

The increased vitality achieved in the case study areas was also considered a benefit, with the mix of uses at Waterfront and Castle Wharf seen as important in making these places destinations in their own right. At Brindleyplace, the designers argued that a true mix of uses had not been achieved because of institutional and planning problems and that more housing could have increased vitality.

On environmental issues, designers looked to their clients to take the lead. In turn, developers looked to their own clients – potential occupiers – when making judgements. For this reason, only those buildings where occupiers demanded energy efficiency were actively designed to reduce environmental impact. These included buildings at Brindleyplace, Waterfront, Castle Wharf and Standard Court and the entire development at Barbirolli Square. Nevertheless, all designers believed the urban design of their schemes to have had a positive impact on the local environment – through regenerating the canalside and building at higher densities at Brindleyplace and Castle Wharf; through putting in place what might in future become a town centre and introducing extensive soft landscaping at Waterfront; and generally through bringing brownfield sites back into use.

6.5 Occupiers' perspectives

Occupiers' perspectives on economic value

Occupiers divided into those for whom urban design was an important factor (generally found in the higher rated cases studies) and those for whom urban design was not a primary consideration (generally found in the lower rated developments). The latter group were significantly less happy about their work environment, for example at Waterfront where poor connections with the surrounding area, limited amenities and the impossibility of walking to work were seen as distinct disadvantages. For this type of occupier, locational factors were decisive. Such factors included

- the quality of the office space itself and its cost (at Exchange Quay, for example, occupiers saw the development as secure and cheap)

- distance from the previous location. A desire not to disturb staff commuting patterns was shared by many – although not all – occupiers, especially those at Castle Wharf and Barbirolli Square.

Unsurprisingly, the commercial deal was an important factor in decision-making for all occupiers. One former occupier at Exchange Quay had moved to Barbirolli Square when their favourable lease had come to an end and they realised that they could move to a superior environment and location for a comparable deal. In this case, the move was characterised as a 'quality of life' issue. For occupiers in developments with superior urban design attributes, urban design quality was important in their choice of location, although they did not talk about it in these terms. Instead they talked of seeking a 'good ambience' or a 'congenial up and coming environment', or 'somewhere staff would be happy'. Occupiers at Castle Wharf were keen to find an attractive, mixed use environment, while an occupier in Barbirolli Square mentioned the 'how many minutes to Marks and Spencer test'.

All occupiers were happy with the levels of rent they were paying and agreed that a better designed environment could and should command increased rents. Occupiers at Barbirolli Square were aware, for instance, that they were paying at the top end of the market but reflected the prevalent attitude that you pay for what you get – an attitude that extends to better quality environments as well as to better quality buildings. They were not, however, prepared to pay more for what they saw as architectural fripperies such as glass lifts and architectural fashion statements. At Waterfront, the perception was that the uniqueness of the development in the area commanded higher rental levels, whilst at Castle Wharf occupiers believed that both architectural and urban design quality added value. Conversely, at Exchange Quay the prevailing attitude was summed up by one occupier who described the development as 'just an estate on the edge of Manchester', adding that they did not expect to pay extra for the environment on offer. At Standard Court, the feeling was that the development had not lived up to its potential and that the urban design problems were now influencing the move away from commercial to residential accommodation on the site.

Prestige and image were important factors for occupiers, particularly those with predominantly UK based businesses whose clients frequently visited. Occupiers at Brindleyplace, Barbirolli Square, Castle Wharf and to a lesser extent Waterfront rated their developments highly and were proud to invite clients to their offices. Clients had been positive about each of the developments and staff at Castle Wharf were able to schedule more meetings at their own offices, with associated time savings. Occupiers at Brindleyplace reflected that in an age of e-commerce, the modern environment in and around their offices gave clients the right message. At Standard Court, private occupiers were critical of the image created, although the Health Authority were pleased that they had been able to re-occupy the refurbished and historic former hospital buildings. For them, however, the on-street parking in and around the entrance to their offices gave an unwelcoming impression to clients.

Occupiers were mainly content with operational performance, although they were consistently critical at Standard Court about the skateboarder problems. Waterfront suffered from a wind tunnel effect down the centre of the development and the buildings themselves were considered costly to heat and cool.

Perhaps most significantly, however, evidence was offered that the better designed environments beneficially impacted on the productivity and the health and satisfaction of the workforce. At Brindleyplace and Barbirolli Square, the design of the surrounding environment was directly credited with increasing the productivity of the workforce, in large part due to the happier work environment created. At Castle Wharf, two of the larger organisations had surveyed their workforce and found that health and satisfaction was better, absenteeism and staff turnover less and productivity higher. Urban design and the mix of uses and facilities both on-site and in the immediate vicinity of the development were considered important factors in this change, which was seen as saving resources in reduced training for new staff. In the less highly rated case studies, although occupiers were happy with performance levels, positive views on health and satisfaction were not forthcoming, although new buildings had helped to rationalise staffing arrangements.

Occupiers' perspectives on social and environmental value

For occupiers, the urban design rating of developments broadly reflected the social value perceived to be added. So, for example, occupiers at Brindleyplace, Barbirolli Square and Castle Wharf believed their developments to be attractive and well integrated into their surroundings, particularly in urban design terms (if not always architecturally), whilst occupiers at Waterfront perceived the development to be attractive if poorly integrated into the neighbouring settlement of Brierley Hill. Occupiers in Standard Court and Exchange Quay were critical of their work environments on both counts.

All occupiers felt that the case study developments contributed to some extent towards a new identity for their areas: Waterfront was seen as adding something new to the Black Country, Exchange Quay as providing a landmark through height and colour, Castle Wharf as providing a 'wow factor' and Barbirolli Square as offering new cultural facilities. However, such impacts were not always viewed positively. Standard Court was seen as not valuing the historical associations of its site, Waterfront was blamed for ruining Brierley Hill town centre and the regeneration impact of Exchange Quay was not considered to have trickled down to the local community – workers commuted from all over the region but rarely from the local area.

Vitality was also seen as a two-sided coin, generally being valued where it existed but also seen as a potential distraction for workers where it did not. At Standard Court, occupiers were generally keen to preserve a peaceful working environment, despite criticising the arena as unpopular. At Brindleyplace, Barbirolli Square and Castle Wharf vitality was seen as a major benefit of the urban design solution, whilst Exchange Quay was characterised by one occupier as 'a soulless out of town estate'. There, and to a lesser extent at Waterfront, the lack of variety in facilities and amenities was criticised. By contrast, the mix of uses available in the more central case studies (with the exception of Standard Court) was enjoyed by occupiers, particularly the fine grained mix of leisure and retail uses available at Castle Wharf.

The broadly inclusive nature of these developments was also valued, although at Brindleyplace some concerns were expressed about gentrification and occupiers were doubtful that all sections of society would be welcomed. Waterfront and Exchange Quay were also regarded as exclusionary, the first because of its isolation and the type of clientele attracted to the bars and the second because of an active exclusion policy.

Occupiers confirmed the disconnection of the lower rated developments from their surroundings but attributed this to location rather than design. Good pedestrian access and connections with surrounding areas were valued in the more central schemes, as was relatively good access by public transport. Conversely, the congestion caused by the out of town schemes was lamented. Parking provision (or the lack of it) was seen as a problem by all occupiers.

Safety was also prioritised by occupiers. Whereas in and around Barbirolli Square the safety of the area was perceived to have dramatically improved, bringing with it real social benefits, at Exchange Quay the feeling of safety did not extend beyond the gates and security guards. Thus although in all developments safety was maintained by security arrangements of varying visibility, in the three higher rated developments the degree of activity around the clock extended the benefits to a wider area. In each of these developments the urban design solution was seen as the major factor in adding social value to the community, while in the other developments design was seen to create social costs.

Occupiers largely confirmed most investors' views that for the majority of companies environmental issues are not a major consideration. Only BT at Castle Wharf had considered the issue in moving to their new building, ensuring – in line with their corporate policy – that a good BREEAM rating was secured. All other occupiers indicated that such concerns had not been considered when moving and only one indicated that they had since become a concern and would be considered in their next move. Nevertheless, most companies believed that the developments they occupied contributed in some way to improving the local environment, even if only through the clearance of contaminated land. Nevertheless, those developments with less successful urban design solutions were generally more heavily criticised in this area as well as on other issues. For example, occupiers at Standard Court were disappointed that the development had not made more of the opportunities provided by its location next to Nottingham Castle.

At Standard Court and the other more urban developments, access to public transport was seen as a boon which in some instances had an environmental benefit by reducing car usage. The belated arrival of the tram to Exchange Quay was also valued, although established travel patterns had not significantly changed. The greatest problems were experienced at Waterfront, where occupiers reported that a private car was necessary and said that accessibility problems had even caused recruitment difficulties.

Issues of greenery and ecology were not such readily apparent concerns, with occupiers seeing landscape as largely an aesthetic concern. Occupiers in Exchange Quay, for example, valued the landscaping in the development but saw it as 'an office with a bit of greenery outside' rather than an attempt to be 'green'. Most occupiers felt that in urban situations, issues of ecology and greening were of little real concern.

6.6 Local authority (planning and economic development) perspectives

Local authority perspectives on economic value

For the planning authorities (and the former Urban Development Corporations operating in Manchester and Salford), the main objective of all the case study developments had been to bring back into viable use areas which had suffered decline and to rectify problems caused by insensitive development in the recent past.

Thus the subtext to all the developments (whether well designed or not) was either the creation of jobs or the levering in of planning gain. Most of the developments had attracted significant private sector resources into their areas and some had received grants from the European Union which were conditional on the delivery of key social as well as economic benefits. The provision of new public spaces in Manchester and Nottingham helped to satisfy these conditions. All the case study developments had helped to create jobs, although authorities were unconvinced that many of these were new jobs as opposed to relocations. Nevertheless, at Castle Wharf, the provision of a high quality environment had helped to persuade the Nottingham Evening Post to stay in the city centre. This was regarded as a major coup for the city and bolstered the planning authority's new emphasis on urban design.

In Manchester, Nottingham and Birmingham the regeneration that the developments helped to bring was considered durable. In Dudley and Salford, significant further infrastructure was still being put in place (to which the initial developers had not contributed) to ensure the regeneration benefits endured. This imposed major costs on the public purse (and in Dudley on the new owners of the development as well).

For some authorities (particularly Birmingham), urban design was seen as a primary means to meet regeneration objectives, while for others (particularly the former Urban Development Corporations (UDCs)), urban design was not a primary consideration. Most authorities perceived their key role as pulling together the various parties to make things happen and to encourage regeneration.

For most, there was also a sense that the new developments carried a greater prestige than the market norm in their areas. This derived from good building design and urban design but also from the 'newness' factor. In Dudley, evidence that rental and market values had risen had been observed, a factor put down partly to the absence of similar high specification offices in the area but also to the new urban design framework emerging through the UDP. In Nottingham and Salford property values had also risen, although because of the regeneration effects rather than necessarily because of the urban design.

A key concern of authorities was that developments should set a standard and open up opportunities for other developments. This has clearly happened in Birmingham and Nottingham. In Salford, however, the local authority argued that Exchange Quay effectively set back the regeneration of Salford Quays by soaking up much of the initial office demand into an isolated and introspective development. At Waterfront, the main urban design framework was being supported by the current owner precisely because of the development opportunities it opened up.

In terms of place marketing, the higher rated developments in each case study pair have been a significant boon to their respective cities. Planning officers in Nottingham went so far as to claim that good urban design is now seen as a means to give the city a competitive edge. The developments have also brought about the reintroduction of housing into Birmingham city centre, the funding of public realm improvements in Manchester and the cross-funding of Bridgewater Hall, as well as improvements to connectivity in Nottingham's south side. In Dudley, a general failure to design at a strategic level ensured that a new monorail system was never fully viable and today is no longer used. This significant (and ongoing) cost illustrates the potential costs of less successful urban design solutions, as does the underused arena at the heart of the Standard Court development.

Officers dismissed the notion that good design took longer to secure planning permission. Indeed, the Castle Wharf, Brindleyplace and Barbirolli Square developments had all received initial permissions quickly because of their perceived good design and regeneration impacts. Furthermore, it was agreed that in all three developments, the early and continuing close involvement of the planning authority helped to ensure high quality design solutions. Regrettably, beyond the immediate control of the main developer, the construction of Castle Wharf was subject to delays following attempts by the design and build contractor of the Evening Post building to cut back on the design specification that had received planning permission. The move resulted in enforcement action, delay and a court case.

Local authority perspectives on social and environmental value

The added social value produced by the higher rated developments in each case study pair came through clearly in the views of planning officers. Brindleyplace, Castle Wharf and Barbirolli Square were perceived to be attractive, welcoming and well-integrated developments, possessing vitality and enhancing local facilities and amenities.

The other developments were not rated so highly in the social value they offered because of their disconnectedness and/or lack of vitality. Despite the aspiration of Nottingham planners that Standard Court should provide a new and vital public space, they have since accepted that the mix of uses was wrong and that the square was unlikely ever to offer broader social value except as a host to very occasional events. Waterside, however, despite its relative disconnection, has proved a major draw for the younger car-borne community.

The final major perceived benefit from the developments at Brindleyplace, Castle Wharf and Barbirolli Square which did not apply to their pairs was the reintegration of parts of cities into the established urban grain and the opening up of areas from which the public was once excluded. Each had become detached because of recent dereliction and insensitive provision of infrastructure and, although it was conceded that none of the case studies had completely resolved these problems, each went a long way to reconnecting their city centres with their hinterland. The boost this had given the cities – both in the provision of new and attractive places to be and in the recivilisation of their urban centres – could not, it was argued, be underestimated. Enhanced civic pride was the key social outcome.

In environmental terms, the case studies revealed a remarkably consistent picture. The major environmental gain (and therefore value) claimed by all planning authorities was the beneficial reuse of derelict and frequently contaminated sites. At the same time, none of the authorities had prioritised, at the beginning of each development, issues of energy consumption or green space provision. (The latter concern was again not generally considered relevant in highly urban contexts.) A number of planning officers commented that environmental issues had only recently come onto the agenda. Besides a general concern to relate schemes to the built heritage, ecological considerations did not feature in decision-making processes.

Accessibility and traffic generation concerns were considered by a range of planning authorities. At Waterfront and Exchange Quay, authorities reported a considerable environmental cost as a direct result of the failure to integrate public transport from the outset. In the other case studies, no direct cost was reported.

6.7   Users' perspectives

Users' perspectives on economic value

The perception of users was largely dependent on the kind and intensity of their own use of the public spaces in the developments. Daily users of the spaces – mostly office workers from the surrounding buildings – tended to gauge the value added as a function of the benefits added to their working environments. Thus users valued the proximity of restaurants and shops and the existence of safe and well-maintained open spaces as meeting places and spaces in which to relax during work breaks. Occasional users and visitors – more frequent in the most centrally located cases but also at Waterfront (and never at Exchange Quay) – tended to relate value to the improvement of available facilities and amenities in a wider context.

Nearly all users agreed that the main economic value added by the developments was the creation of jobs, especially in the office sector but also in the leisure industry. The transformation of derelict sites into business locations was also perceived to be a major benefit. Nevertheless, neither gain was necessarily considered to be the result of urban design quality, although interestingly the attractiveness of developments was implicitly linked to the quantity and quality of the jobs they provided. The success of these developments as employment generators was also linked by many to their prestige as office locations.

Occasional users emphasised the economic impact that developments had in their regions. Beyond the creation of jobs, developments were sometimes seen as instrumental in projecting a new, economically dynamic image of their cities to the outside world. Thus Brindleyplace was described as 'putting Birmingham back on the map' and Castle Wharf as bringing more people (including tourists) into the heart of Nottingham and providing custom for local shops.

However, some users expressed doubts about the degree to which some of these economic benefits would impact on neighbouring communities. This was especially true in the more inward-looking and insular developments (Exchange Quay, Standard Court and to a lesser extent Waterfront).

Users' perspectives on social and environmental value

For users, the main social value came in the contribution that nearly all the developments made to the provision of leisure facilities and amenities, including new public spaces and landscaped areas. A good proportion of users interviewed at Brindleyplace, Barbirolli Square, Castle Wharf and – more surprisingly in the light of its relative isolation – Waterfront were there for specific leisure purposes, taking advantage of the bars, cafes or simply the open spaces. By contrast the users interviewed at Exchange Quay were all office workers. At Standard Court, despite visiting twice on a sunny day, the researchers found no one other than the occasional worker passing through the main space.

Some users commented on the perceived exclusivity of developments, including some of the well-integrated higher rated case studies (Brindleyplace and Barbirolli Square). There was a trade-off between feeling safe and the perception of being in a 'privatised' public realm. Those working in the developments did not see exclusivity as a problem for themselves although many acknowledged that it might intimidate others.

Users saw places that were vital and well-used throughout the day as safer. The Waterfront development scored highly here because of its thriving night-time economy. It also managed to draw in some shoppers from the neighbouring Merry Hill shopping centre looking for an open-air leisure space. Castle Wharf benefited from similar activity. On the other hand, those developments with limited uses or where uses were spatially segregated were perceived as safe during office hours but less so in the evenings or at weekends. Brindleyplace and to a greater extent Standard Court came into this category.

Users in Brindleyplace, Castle Wharf and Barbirolli Square all defined the developments as pleasant and attractive. This was linked to design qualities including

■ trees, water and sculptures in Brindleyplace

■ a sense of seclusion, peace and quiet in Barbirolli Square (although the lack of maintenance was criticised)

■ the canal and leisure facilities at Castle Wharf.

The less successful developments in urban design terms were seen as good only in comparison with their surroundings; for example, Exchange Quay was described as an 'oasis in run-down surroundings' but was criticised for its overall quality. The wind-tunnel effect was mentioned by more than one user, as was the failure to relate the canal to the development. At Standard Court, the lack of greenery and the poor integration of the development with its surroundings were raised as concerns. The exception was Waterfront where the successful landscaping and integration of the canal, as well as the integration of the leisure facilities along the canalside, provided a pleasant and much appreciated environment.

In some of the developments, users valued the improved accessibility to those parts of their cities opened up by the developments. This was particularly true at Castle Wharf and to a lesser extent at Barbirolli Square, where users regretted the remaining localised problems with connectivity.

Most users also perceived the higher ranking developments to have dealt with the natural environment more successfully. However, planting was sometimes criticised as obviously placed and artificial. Treatment of canals was often seen as the main determinant of how well the natural environment had been integrated in developments; Castle Wharf, Brindleyplace and Waterfront were considered to have managed this most successfully and Exchange Quay least successfully. At Standard Court, the lack of any greenery was criticised.

In general, all the developments were seen by users as contributing to some degree to local congestion, with those less centrally located or poorly served by public transport identified as the main culprits. However, most users noted that the developments drew from a large catchment area and therefore required car use. Deficient connections in the public transport system seemed to contribute to the decision of many people to drive to work.

Nearly all the developments were regarded by their users as pedestrian friendly. For the centrally located and more integrated developments, this tended to mean that once off the surrounding major roads, users found it relatively easy to walk around unencumbered by traffic and to reach other areas on foot. For the more insular developments, however, it meant that once access by car had been negotiated through busy roads, the walk to work (or to the leisure facilities at Waterfront) was relatively traffic-free, but that walking anywhere else was difficult. Users at Waterfront acknowledged that newcomers might have a different impression of how easy it was to move around, either by car or on foot.

7.0 Detailed Conclusions

7.1 The literature and research review

THE review revealed a small but growing body of international research concerned with the relationship between design and value. Significantly, this research consistently concluded that good urban design added economic value in the form of better value for money, higher asset exchange value and better lifecycle value. It suggested that good urban design could confer social and environmental value and provide long-term economic spin-offs in the wider economy from regenerative effects.

The combined research also suggested that good urban design is not necessarily expensive or unaffordable and that on the balance of costs and benefits it makes economic sense to invest in good design. The initial findings also confirmed that this value can be measured using qualitative and quantitative methodologies.

The review suggested that good urban design should be promoted because of its capacity to add value.

7.2 The empirical research: economic value

Does good urban design add economic value?

Broadly the empirical evidence suggests that good urban design does add economic value. All groups of stakeholders concurred with this conclusion although not all interviewees agreed on what constituted good urban design.

Based on the research evidence it can be concluded that

- good urban design delivers economic value through returning high profits for owners and investors

- this is most clear and direct in those parts of the market where environmental quality is a major concern – the higher end of the market – although at the lower end good urban design can still deliver economic value

- because good urban design often occurs in pioneering development, enhanced profits can be delayed, leaving developers who sell out early under-compensated for their risk

- occupiers seem to benefit from productivity gains, increased prestige and a happier workforce

- area regeneration based on good urban design delivers a clear economic dividend to society.

Urban design and economic value

- Design (including urban design) was seen as important to the delivery of all types of commercial office environment, from those which rate well in urban design terms to those that are not so highly rated.

- In some cases, design is viewed primarily as a means to create a particular type of corporate image and environment. This may not rate well in urban design terms but is nevertheless a carefully conceived and designed product.

- Occupier attitudes seem to be the key to delivering quality.

- Occupiers for whom urban design is not a concern and for whom decisions are based primarily on cost, location and office specification show more discontent with the environments they end up occupying.

■ High quality urban design is attractive to key sections of the rental, investment and owner/occupier market, who are prepared to pay extra for better quality design.

■ All occupiers accept that better quality environments (like any other form of superior product) can and should command increased rents.

■ Good urban design tends to be reflected in high levels of rent and in higher investment returns, at least over the medium- to long-term.

■ Quality is seen as relative to what is already available in any given market or geographic area. Thus not every development needs to be a Brindleyplace to command higher rents, but does need to raise the quality of its urban design above that generally offered in the area.

Delivery of economic value

■ Investment decisions are dominated by economic and locational concerns but urban design is still a major factor; faced with otherwise comparable developments, occupiers may decide on the basis of urban design quality.

■ In this context, design was important in all the case studies as a means to attract a particular market.

■ The ability to recognise the gap in the market and to design suitable, flexible accommodation seems most influential in determining vacancy rates.

■ Urban design solutions seem to represent a compromise between clear commercial objectives and the public objectives of the local authority, with the best urban design solutions resulting when these two sets of objectives coincide – preferably from inception.

■ The early and focused intervention of the public sector is crucial in steering developments beyond purely commercial concerns to the delivery of good urban design.

■ Public sector land ownership (although not gap funding) plays a key role in getting the best out of sites. The higher rated case studies were all on sites owned by local authorities.

■ A lack of public sector guidance, together with an uncertain or risky commercial context, tends to deliver lower quality urban design solutions (two of the three less successfully designed case studies occurred against a background of minimal local authority input).

The private economic benefits of good urban design

■ Good urban design raises capital and rental values.

■ Good urban design places developments at the higher end of the rental market and, as long as demand exists for this type of accommodation, such developments seem to have little difficulty filling their space.

■ Good urban design supports the 'life giving' uses in developments (cafes, shops, pubs, etc.), elements which were seen as important in projecting a contemporary image and in attracting occupiers.

■ Good urban design helps define the place and location, primarily through raising the profile of developments.

■ Good urban design allows developers to break into new markets and to expand their businesses by creating high profile, clearly recognisable products.

■ Many of the best urban design developments are pioneering in nature, opening up new areas for commercial development.

■ Such developments are more difficult to finance in the first place and only slowly unleash the regenerative effects that subsequently add value to the pioneering scheme. If initial developers are to benefit from the healthy financial returns that such developments can offer in the medium- to long-term, they need to retain a stake after completion.

■ Good urban design helps to enhance investor confidence in innovative developments on more marginal sites. Good urban design can help to pre-let (and therefore finance) such development.

■ Good urban design can help to deliver more development (and therefore more lettable floor area) by enabling building at higher densities.

■ For occupiers, good urban design was seen to enhance company image.

■ Companies occupying better designed (particularly mixed-use) environments report increased health and satisfaction amongst their workforces and reduced absenteeism and staff turnover.

■ This can lead to increased productivity, time saved through more meetings scheduled in-house and reduced staff recruitment and training costs.

The public economic benefits of good urban design

■ Good urban design can inspire physical and social regeneration by generating confidence, thereby attracting further development and raising property prices.

■ Good urban design can help to create jobs (mainly through mixing uses) and can be decisive in retaining companies in particular areas (and in urban as opposed to out of town locations).

■ If clearly linked to the delivery of social and economic objectives, the delivery of high quality public spaces can also help to attract European Union and other grant monies.

■ Good urban design is widely featured in public sector place marketing campaigns and is seen as giving cities a competitive and dynamic image.

■ Good urban design can help ensure sustainable regeneration. Conversely, poor urban design can undermine regeneration efforts and place a considerable financial burden on the public sector in the long run.

■ The design quality of development is perceived by users to be linked to the quality and quantity of jobs created.

The economic costs of good urban design

■ No evidence was found that the purchase of low value or subsidised land or development opportunities was essential for the delivery of good urban design.

■ No evidence was found that good urban design raised design or development costs.

■ No evidence was found that good urban design increased the length of time taken to secure planning permission.

■ Conservation controls were however found to raise design times, construction costs (through higher quality materials and finishes) and therefore overall development costs, as well as the time taken to secure detailed consents.

■ Good urban design can reduce security, management, maintenance and energy costs. Nevertheless, when associated with the provision of new public spaces, such costs need to be supported by enough critical mass (of development) to avoid becoming a burden on investors or – via service charges – on occupiers.

■ Management and maintenance costs are not a major consideration in the development process. Indeed, the economic relationships and priorities in the system still tend to be driven by short-term considerations.

The economic costs of poor urban design

■ Poor urban design can undermine amenities delivered through planning gain, in the worst cases turning them into liabilities rather than public benefits.

■ The failure to deliver connected, well-integrated environments imposes costs which later have to be borne by public and private stakeholders, although original developers have often moved on.

■ Poor urban design at the larger spatial scale (relating to connectivity and infrastructure) limits investment opportunities.

■ Poor urban design seems to reduce the extent to which and the speed at which the regenerative impacts of development ripple through local economies.

7.3 The empirical research: environmental and social value

Does good urban design add environmental and social value?

The research makes a clear case that good urban design adds social value. Each group of stakeholders confirmed this from their own perspective.

The environmental case was less clear cut because of the poor understanding of environmental issues. Partly in consequence, none of the case study developments had comprehensively dealt with them, making measurement of their impact difficult. Nevertheless, where environmental issues were actively addressed (or at least considered) by stakeholders, the research showed that good urban design delivered distinct environmental value.

Urban design and social value

■ In places where development opportunities are in short supply, almost any development offers social value – of sorts – and therefore all the developments examined provided some degree of social value through their regenerative impact and potential for job creation.

■ Some urban design solutions enhance the social benefits that development brings, spreading them to a broader geographic area and population.

■ Some poor urban design solutions (e.g. introspective, exclusive and disconnected urban environments) limit the spread of social benefits from developments and may even create social (and economic) costs.

■ Social value was seen as a broad concept that should rightfully spread beyond the boundaries of a particular site, requiring that development should be designed to integrate into its surroundings.

■ Not all stakeholders share the notion that development should deliver social value beyond its immediate physical regenerative impact. In this sense, urban design quality is primarily influenced by commercial development aspirations which sometimes – but not always – coincide with public aspirations.

■ These aspirations most often coincide when higher rental returns are sought through building high quality products for the top end of the market.

■ The attitudes of occupiers and the quality for which they are willing to pay largely determines the attitudes of developers and investors to delivering better urban design.

Delivery of social benefits

■ Achieving better urban design seems to be more of a concern in established urban contexts, although this does not necessarily guarantee enhanced social value. Outside such contexts, critical mass seems to be required to deliver broader social value.

■ Private sector activity alone has great difficulty delivering the full range of positive. social impacts that well designed development can deliver.

■ The market has difficulty delivering the kind of truly fine-grained mixed-use development which adds the most social value.

■ Mix of uses and design and positioning of public spaces should be realistic and reflect both the location and accessibility of the site and its constituent parts.

The social benefits of good urban design

■ Good urban design helps to deliver more contextually integrated development, even when architectural solutions remain strictly corporate in nature.

■ Good urban design can provide the means to open up areas and amenities.

■ Good urban (and architectural) design – particularly well-designed public spaces – helps to boost city pride.

■ Good urban design enhances social inclusiveness by cutting down on the need for high profile security arrangements.

■ Good urban design and the associated increased vitality increase feelings of safety both within sites and beyond them.

- Varied uses and facilities are valued by occupiers and where they do not exist they are missed. Nevertheless, in working environments a balance is important between vitality and peace and quiet.

- If well designed and located, comfortable new public open spaces and their associated facilities can greatly add to the sense of social well-being and civic pride.

- For users (workers and visitors), social value is most clearly identified with the provision of facilities and amenities and pleasant places in which to use them.

- Physical design, distribution of uses and levels of activity during the day and at night directly determine the degree to which non-occupiers feel welcome in developments, and therefore perceptions of exclusivity.

The social costs of good urban design

- Gentrification was the only identified social cost linked to improving the environment, as marginal uses and lifestyles are dislocated from regenerated areas.

- Significantly, good urban design can actively encourage gentrification by spreading economic and social benefits over a wider area.

The social costs of poor urban design

- Exclusionary and disconnected environments are not valued by any stakeholders, although locational rather than urban design factors were considered the primary cause of these deficiencies.

- Physical disconnection disproportionately impacts on the opportunities available to the less mobile.

- Disconnection from public transport networks and established urban areas can cause staff recruitment and retention problems.

- Social value is not delivered by the provision of public open space if that space is poorly integrated with its environment. In some circumstances, social value can be diminished by poorly designed public space.

- Public spaces have different qualities and purposes which should be reflected in their design. Such spaces should not serve as short-term means to attract grant monies.

Urban design and environmental value

- The delivery of good urban design is associated with the delivery of more environmentally supportive development.

- Where dereliction and decay are rife, almost all development can be viewed as an environmental gain.

- Recycling of derelict and contaminated land and the removal of unwanted buildings offers environmental benefits in perceptual, aesthetic and sometimes ecological terms, although resulting developments do not always enhance this value.

- Poor urban design solutions - particularly those poorly integrated into the public transport infrastructure – can produce environmental degradation that is even more intense (if less visible).

Delivery of environmental benefits

- Investment and development companies operating at the higher end of the market are beginning to support the notion that environmentally supportive development offers increased economic value over the longer term.

- Few stakeholders understand the potential environmental contribution of good urban design, beyond the impact of land recycling and the construction of more energy efficient buildings.

- Environmental benefits were only considered and delivered in response to perceived occupier demand.

- Such demand existed primarily at the higher end of the market, as environmental measures increase up-front construction costs which are reflected in rents demanded from occupiers.

- The research detected some evidence that environmental concerns are increasingly on the agenda of occupiers, although concern starts from a very low base.

The environmental benefits of good urban design

- Where provided, environmentally supportive (or at least energy efficient) development offered a means to attract 'blue chip' tenants – although so did internal environmental control and increased parking standards.

- Parking concerns were fundamental across all markets. Under-provision had severe consequences for both occupancy rates and rental values.

- So, to a lesser extent, did integration with public transport networks, which was deemed to offer a clear competitive advantage to developments.

- Accessible, centrally located developments were considered to be less environmentally costly than out of town developments.

- Good urban design offered the opportunity to revitalise and better utilise (often ex-industrial) heritage.

- Contextual integration was among the major concerns of everyday users of developments, particularly integration with important structural and natural features such as waterways.

- A greater concern for environmental issues – particularly access, walkability and heritage revitalisation – reinforces social value.

8.0 Recommendations for Further Research

THE present work is not definitive. The study was limited in that it looked at only six predominantly office-based environments in three regional markets. It should therefore be seen as a step towards clarifying the relationship between urban design and value and as a contribution towards future research.

Nonetheless, the present research confirms many of the theoretical costs and benefits of good urban design identified from the literature and research review and presented in Tables 3 and 4. The conclusions presented here are consistent with the findings of related UK and international research in this area and it is expected that they would be substantiated by further work.

There are three particular lines of enquiry where further research would be beneficial. These are a quantitative study of the economic value added by good urban design, a comparative examination of policy mechanisms associated with the delivery of good urban design and research into a possible method for measuring the value added by new developments.

A quantitative study of the economic value of good urban design: work in the USA and Australia (Annex A) shows how a more precise correlation can be established between design qualities and indicators of economic performance. At present there is no equivalent study in the UK, despite the fact that the main inputs for such work are available. This kind of research would be invaluable as a tool for informing private investment decisions in urban design.

A quantitative study of a large sample of similar types of developments (e.g. office-based or retail-based complexes), covering the variety of regional property markets in the UK, could be undertaken. These developments would be classified against design criteria similar to the ones used in the current research (see Figure 2), and their economic performance would be measured in terms of capital values, rents and yields in the context of their respective regional markets over time. The findings would make apparent any correlation between urban design quality and its components and the performance of developments as assets for investors – provided that adequate methodological precautions are taken to isolate other variables that might influence development performance.

A comparative study of policy mechanisms: research on the value added by good urban design should seek to provide tools for persuading the public and private stakeholders involved in the production and management of urban areas that a concern for good design is necessary. Whereas for private interests this might mean demonstrating that good design influences financial returns, for the public sector it would mean not only highlighting the social and environmental benefits of good urban design but also evaluating the possible mechanisms that can be used by local authorities or central government to shape the attitudes and decision-making processes of private stakeholders. For the latter, a comparative analysis of best practice is essential.

A comparative study of urban design quality and the policy mechanisms associated with its delivery could be undertaken. The study would be based on similar types of developments featuring good urban design and located in selected European countries (e.g. France, the UK, the Netherlands, Spain and Sweden). It would focus on the policies influencing design quality and on how these shape the decision-making processes of private sector stakeholders. Replicability and transferability would be important considerations in evaluating different policy tools. Such a study would ideally be developed in collaboration with local research institutions in the countries concerned.

A method for measuring the potential design value of development proposals: the research indicated that beyond standard (and inevitably crude) valuation techniques, no method yet exists to measure the value added by good urban design in new development. The result is that the value added by good design can be sidelined or not considered at all. A tool would be useful to inform decision-making and post-development evaluations.

Such tools already exist in the transport field to value the impact of different infrastructure proposals – particularly new roads. A research project aiming to produce a similar tool for urban design would need to examine these and any that exist in other policy areas (both in the UK and overseas). Extensive (live) case study work would be required to test and refine the tool.

Annexes

A: Qualitative and Quantitative Approaches to Measuring Value in the Built Environment

A1.1 Qualitative approaches

THE most comprehensive of the qualitative-type studies undertaken in the UK is the RICS & DoE (1996) funded study (see Section 4.7) on the way investors, developers and occupiers view urban design quality and the costs and benefits associated with it. Its main focus was on how those stakeholders view the need to invest in urban design quality, the rationale for their views, and how they have done so in a number of empirical cases.

As the research showed, design quality emerges as the result of the attitude of developers, investors and occupiers to the perceived balance between the associated costs, benefits and risks. However, the balance is different for each of those stakeholders, and might vary with time. Moreover, the nature of the development process itself and the dynamics of the various sectors of the property market condition how the balance works out, with some stakeholders favouring an 'appropriate' view of design quality (i.e. the minimum necessary to secure that a development is bought or leased, or that it can accommodate a particular use), whereas for others it makes sense to invest in better quality (the 'sustainable' quality view).

The study did not aim to assess the value of good urban design directly. However, it did examine how design quality is taken into account by developers, investors and occupiers and how it is weighed against other concerns in their decision-making. It showed how value is assessed by the main participants in a development according to their own specific range of considerations. This 'qualitative look' at the value of good urban design provides a framework for comparing better design with those other considerations within the development process as it is currently organised, and for identifying the main variables determining the value of better design for each player. What this suggests is that the value of better design is to some extent relative, a function of interacting hierarchies of considerations applied by developers, investors and occupiers, each with their own rationale. Moreover, it can vary with changes in both the structure of those hierarchies and the nature of their interaction.

A similar approach was adopted by Guy (1998) in a piece of research on how environmentally sensitive practices filter through the development process. His main concern was with environmental innovations and property development, while design was briefly examined for its role in delivering better environmental qualities. Through a number of case studies, the research explored how development stakeholders view and value buildings and their qualities, as well as the logic underpinning their views. Design was shown as the material outcome of complex negotiations between the stakeholders seeking to extract different forms of value (financial, cultural, utilitarian, etc.) in the context of wider technical, legal and commercial constraints.

As in the RICS & DoE research, the value of good design – in this case environmentally sound design – was seen as a 'relational' concept, defined through the forms of value sought by competing stakeholders and by the process of interaction between them. The concern was not with an absolute measurement of value but with the processes through which stakeholders change their perception of value and how this informs design practices. As regards design-related environmental innovations, the drivers behind those processes of change include "the need for organisational flexibility of occupiers, the desire to visually symbolise more 'caring' values, concern over sick buildings, and the requirement for less alienating working spaces" (Guy, 1988, p3).

This 'relational' view of how value is created and distributed in the development process was tackled from a different perspective by Verhage and Needham (1997). Their focus was on how housing development quality is determined by negotiations around planning gain, and how the different organisation of the Dutch and British planning systems influence the outcomes. Their main argument was that the distribution of the costs of environmental quality varied according to the degree and type of power over juridical instruments, economic resources and information held by the main stakeholders in the development process. For urban design, the research implied that design quality depends on the outcomes of a complex interplay of power relations and dependencies embedded in the planning system. Thus, although the study had no explicit concern for how environmental quality can be valued, its findings suggest that the rationales for each stakeholder's view on the value of design (which determines how much they are prepared to invest in it) are mediated by the nature of the system of interaction among those stakeholders, determined by the planning system, market regulations, and so forth.

Worpole (1999) raises the possibility of a mixed approach to the value of better design, incorporating qualitative and quantitative elements. Here the focus was on architectural design, but the conceptual problems are similar. The study did not discuss explicitly how the value added in these areas can be measured, but instead Worpole discusses the areas in which good architecture and design can add value in its widest sense and the processes through which this is done, highlighting the following:

■ the wider economic impacts of attractive buildings and settings in terms of area regeneration

■ the value for money achieved through technical and intellectual expertise applied to buildings and sites

■ the enhancement of individual and social well-being and quality of life brought about by good design

■ adaptability, energy efficiency and environmental sustainability.

The definition of the impact of better design (the areas above) suggests that the value of design has two dimensions. The first is a measurable part accruing either to those directly concerned with the building (e.g. value achieved through optimum use of site or energy efficiency), or to the wider society (e.g. the regenerating impact of flagship developments on the local economy). For this dimension, the study makes its case by referring to findings elsewhere based on performance indicators such as savings in energy consumption, variations in rental values, jobs created, tourist spending in the local economy, and so forth. However, it contends that the impact of better design has often been incremental and therefore has a time dimension that should be considered when assessing its impact.

The second consists of the intangible components which can only be gauged by indirect methods and approximations. These are assessed through the perceptions by relevant stakeholders of the merits of better design and its effects on individual and social well-being. It reveals itself through surveys of factors underpinning locational decisions of occupiers, changes in design practices of developers, recognition of the importance of design by statutory bodies, and indirect statistical measurements (e.g. the increase in footfall in an area). However, these perceptions are linked to assumptions about causal relations between design quality and social and economic processes which are not always easy to demonstrate.

Loe (1999) suggests a similar approach. He describes the various approaches to valuing building qualities (good design being one such quality) used by the construction industry. These range from the mainstream valuation of buildings as tangible assets, to several building rating methods which try to take into account the match between the qualities of a building and the requirements of its occupants, to more recent attempts to assess the wider social impacts of buildings and developments. The main argument was again the existence of directly measurable economic value together with value of a relational nature, which exists as a function of the views and expectations of different stakeholders as defined through their interactions.

A1.2 Quantitative approaches

The emphasis on the measurable impacts of better design is behind the second family of approaches to the value of design. Two methodological key issues underpin these approaches. The first concerns the areas of the economy to which the costs and benefits of better design are most significant, such as property values, job creation and health care (the way it is tackled being dependent upon whose benefits and costs the research is trying to assess). The second concerns how to convert to monetary values the intangible benefits and costs of design (the externalities produced by good design) and simultaneously how to ascribe these to specific stakeholders.

While there have been no attempts in the UK explicitly to value the social, economic and environmental benefits accruing from the impact of better urban design on the public realm in terms of their monetary worth, from an economic stand-point these benefits can – in principle – be valued. Indeed, there are ways of attributing monetary values to such benefits, relying on various established techniques which attempt to do precisely that. For instance, to aid the process of deciding whether to preserve an old building or demolish it to make way for something new, considerations about relative values have to be balanced and quite often decisions are made on the basis of investment appraisals and cost–benefit analyses which give some kind of implied value for the qualities of the older architecture through shadow pricing.

The Property Council of Australia (1999) commissioned research on the added value of good urban design is a good example. The concern was to analyse whether well-designed developments out-perform others from an investor's point of view. The study looked at a small number of cases and compared increases in capital values and rent returns against average local indexes for similar types of property. The findings suggest that well-designed developments have a superior financial performance compared to the average and do not necessarily cost more for the investors.

As important as the study's conclusion – that good design pays financial dividends – is how the conclusion was derived. A key issue was the selection of the case studies, which were based on seven criteria (see Section 4.7). It is not entirely clear what the exact nature of the causality nexus linking the applied criteria to the superior investment performance found in each case was (or how much other variables such as location, timing of development, mix of uses, nature of tenancies, and so forth can explain their performance). However, the use of selection criteria which implicitly value the intangible costs and benefits of superior urban design allowed the study to concentrate the analysis on the straightforward comparison of capital values and rental growth without having to resort to complex methodologies. According to the study's logic, the selected cases represent the highest degree of value for the seven criteria. This was then correlated to investment performance to test whether better urban design produced a higher investment return. Exploring this logic, it would be expected that a decrease in design quality would be related to a decrease in investment performance, something which might or might not be confirmed by a larger research project. The difficulty remained to understand how the benefits and costs involved in producing better design – which concur to produce better investment performance – are distributed amongst key stakeholders, and how this varies over time.

Vandell and Lane (1989) adopted a similar approach to determine the value added by good architectural and urban design through their examination of over one hundred 'type A' office buildings in the USA. Their aim was to detect correlations between good design and a set of indicators of economic performance, chiefly rental values and vacancy rates. The design ratings of the selected buildings (see Section 4.7) were compared against indicators of economic performance for each of the buildings, showing the correlation between variations in design quality and variations in rental values and vacancy rates.

The study showed a positive correlation between design quality and rent (the higher the design rating, the higher the rents), although better design did not seem to affect variations in vacancy rates. Of particular interest were:

■ The attempt to establish a gradation of design quality to test against similar gradations of economic indicators.

■ The results of parallel tests correlating rents with variables such as number of floors, age and so forth. These hinted at a strong interdependence between the subjective preferences of stakeholders at a particular time and the apparently neutral indicators of economic rationality. A positive correlation between high-rise and rent values, for example, could be attributed to subjective perceptions of quality linked to high rise office buildings by particular stakeholders in the mid/late 1980s.

■ That on the basis of a limited database of production costs, the authors suggest that the costs of better design may not be offset by its benefits, particularly from a developer's point of view.

However, the nature of these findings cannot be dissociated from the fact that the definition of good design used throughout the study was very limiting (restricted to aesthetics), which ruled out important dimensions in which there is clear evidence that design adds value, such as functionality.

A more restricted version of this approach to design value was that of Doiron et al (1992), whose concern was with the relationship between rental values and special design features in office buildings. Their study focused on atrium spaces, and using a hedonic pricing model (see below) they defined a curve linking atrium size, rental values and development costs. Using empirical data they concluded that the existence of atria increases rental values, that there is a positive correlation between atrium sizes and rent values up to an optimum point, and that a negative correlation exists between atrium sizes and unit development costs. There was, however, no attempt to examine the quality of design associated with each atrium and in that sense the study also featured a very narrow view on design and value.

An explicitly methodological study of the problems of quantitative valuation in the urban environment can be found in research funded by DNH et al (1996) on the value of heritage conservation. The literature review of the value of conservation in the historic environment concentrates on the various techniques that have been developed to place monetary values on non-traded environmental benefits. Even though these have been so far largely applied in the natural environment, the study suggests that they are also broadly applicable to the assessment of the environmental amenity benefits of conservation and design. The three main kinds of valuation method discussed can be classified on the basis of whether they seek to place a value on a good or attribute directly by determining the willingness of respondents to pay for an improvement in the environmental good or attribute in question or to accept a degradation (contingent valuation), or indirectly by using prices from a related market which already exists (hedonic pricing and travel cost approaches).

The study concluded that in assessing the static benefits of urban conservation, the contingent valuation method is likely to be the most successful, but that the hedonic pricing method might also be useful. These techniques are discussed below, along with a brief discussion of other key valuation techniques – the Delphi technique and cost–benefit analysis.

The hedonic pricing method (HPM) is the most theoretically rigorous of quantitative valuation methods, being strongly rooted in economic theory. It aims to determine the relationship between the attributes of a good and its price and has as its starting point the proposition that any differentiated product has a range of characteristics each with its own implicit (also known as 'shadow') price. Applied to property, it uses econometric analysis of large databases to unbundle environmental attributes from the various other factors making up the price of a dwelling or piece of land.

For housing these differentiated characteristics may be structural (e.g. size of plot, number of bedrooms, availability of a garage or the lack of one) or environmental (e.g. air quality, presence of views, noise levels, or proximity to social amenities) and its price should be seen as the sum of the shadow prices of all its characteristics. Therefore in its price, a given property would reflect – among other things – the quality of the environment in which it is located, while the difference between two identical houses should accurately reflect the consumer's valuation of the marginal difference between attributes such as the presence of double glazing.

This method has been employed in the UK in a planning context in a study using locational as well as structural characteristics in a Hedonic price regression to study the price of housing in Reading and Darlington (Cheshire & Shepherd, 1994). The method allowed for an estimation of how the value of location-specific attributes are capitalised into land prices if these are not included as independent variables. This study included among the variables local amenities provided through the land use planning system.

Other relevant studies that employed this method found that architectural style has a strong impact on the value of residential property (Asabere et al, 1989; Eppli & Tu, 1999), that architecture has certain public good characteristics which may be undervalued in the market (Hough & Kratz, 1983), and that designation of a historic district in Baltimore, USA, positively influenced prices of properties in the area (DNH et al, 1996). See also the outstanding recent work of Cheshire (2000) on the determination of housing prices.

The main difficulty with this approach is that it relies on data from a very large number of cases, and for all the hypothetical explanatory variables themselves to be precisely quantified. To use the method in the current research, the urban features of each case study development would have needed to be measured on a scale to correlate them to variations in the prices of property and much larger numbers of case studies would have been required.

The travel cost method (TCM) uses the time and cost incurred in visiting and enjoying a recreational site (e.g. a site of special historic interest) as a proxy measure of the price of entering it. The visitors' explicit expenditure (expenses on petrol or public transport fares) or implicit expenditure (time spent on the visit) incurred travelling to the site could be used as a measure of their minimum valuation of that site. Also relevant are the opportunity costs (foregone earnings or leisure time which could have been spent on something else).

Past application has mainly been on rural case studies and free-standing attractions, but the method could in principle be applied to urban attractions like historic town centres, scenic botanical gardens in London, cathedrals and so forth which people travel from different parts of the country to visit, some of which might have urban design as part of their attractiveness. It is far more difficult to apply the approach to much more diffuse characteristics of the urban environment such as the amenity or otherwise of a particular office development, and when most journeys are local and associated with other purposes such as travel to work or shopping.

The contingent valuation method (CVM) is the name given to a form of market research where the product is a change in the environment. Thus people are asked directly what their environmental valuations might be, i.e. what they will be willing to pay for a hypothetical environmental improvement or to prevent a deterioration, or what they would be willing to accept in compensation. The CVM may apply equally to changes in 'public goods', such as air quality, landscape/townscape value, or the existence of wildlife, as to goods and services sold to individuals (exchange goods) such as improved water supply and sewerage, all of which might be gains from better urban design.

In contrast to the HPM and the TCM approaches which are indirect methods of eliciting valuations from consumers by considering their revealed consumption in existing related markets, the CVM directly questions consumers on their stated 'willingness to pay' for an environmental improvement, or their 'willingness to accept' compensation for a given fall in the quality of their environment. A key advantage with this method is that since respondents are asked directly about their preferences it is possible to inquire from them their willingness or otherwise to pay for amenities of which they are not direct users. Therefore it is possible to obtain 'option' and 'existence' valuations as well as direct user values (OECD, 1995; DNH et al, 1996).

A direct survey of the users of the public realm could, for example, establish from stakeholders their relative valuation of various improvements, or otherwise, in the quality of environmental services and social amenities that are provided via the design process. Recent decades have witnessed significant growth in the application of this method. Past applications of relevance to urban design outcomes were the valuation of improved park facilities (Combs et al, 1993) and a study by Willis et al (1993) that assessed the usefulness of the CVM as a tool for estimating people's willingness to pay entrance charges to enter Durham Cathedral.

However, as with hedonic pricing, the accuracy of this technique depends on large databases, which translate to analysing the behaviour of large numbers of people in controlled situations. Moreover, there are many subjective judgements of value required from both the researchers and the researched, frequently rending the results open to interpretation. In all these techniques there is also the risk of bias towards the views of high earners, as people with higher levels of income will be prepared to pay more for the enjoyment of a good.

The Delphi technique is another method discussed in DNH et al (1996). Here the views of a panel of experts are sought on their valuation of environmental changes. This is done in preference to depending on expressions of 'willingness to pay' for an environmental improvement or 'willingness to accept' a degradation by individuals who may be irrational, impulsive or poorly informed.

The technique is considered particularly useful where historical data are unavailable or where significant levels of subjective judgement would be necessary. The researcher assembles a diverse team of experts with specialist knowledge of the subject but who are sufficiently independent in their viewpoints to enable subjective valuations. A questionnaire is distributed containing questions on the subject in which their valuation is sought, with the responses analysed and returned to panel members with allowance to alter their views if they wish in the light of other responses. This process is repeated a sufficient number of times before final valuations are reached. This method has the key advantage of being relatively simple; it requires little specialist knowledge on the part of the researcher and is comparatively simple to conduct. However, the researcher needs to guard against biases introduced by the selection of the panel and questionnaire design (Smith, 1989; DNH et al, 1996). To enable meaningful results through an analysis of case studies, significant local knowledge would be required.

Cost benefit–analysis (CBA): the techniques of CBA are, broadly, applicable in the valuation of social costs and benefits in the built environment. They are, for example, used to guide some decisions in the field of urban and regional planning (Snell, 1997), but require sufficient data to be found to aid the numerous calculations necessary to ensure that the evaluation is sufficiently accurate. Unfortunately, severe limitations with this approach mean that decisions can rarely be made on cost–benefit grounds alone, mainly due to the prohibitive cost of finding the appropriate prices and of valuing each alternative in turn. Further limitations include reliance on value judgements and the fact that the CBA must be grounded in a thorough analysis and understanding of the economy of the area concerned and its interactions with the rest of the country. The need to provide simpler, more useful and cost-effective evaluation techniques has led to the development of a number of evaluation methods as adaptations or refinements of CBA.

The planning balance sheet analysis (PBSA) is the closest method to CBA and was explicitly devised to overcome the fact that many social costs and benefits are not easily measured in monetary terms which almost always leaves CBA results subject to charges that some of the costs and benefits were valued incorrectly. Rather than ascribing actual values to costs and benefits, the method merely maps where these should be placed on the balance sheet in terms of assets or liabilities.

PBSA was further developed into community impact analysis (CIA) which indicates which sections of the community are likely to gain or lose from urban planning decisions, thereby taking distributional and efficiency effects into account (Lichfield, 1996). Extensive use is made by environmental psychologists and others of such survey methods which seek directly to elucidate people's values and preferences and the factors which influence their behaviour. The results are non-monetary measures and are often fed into decision-making and evaluation studies. Such studies involve extensive fieldwork, but do have the advantage (over monetary measures) that some quantification is achieved while avoiding the problem of how subjective values convert – if at all – into financial transactions.

The multi-criterion analysis (MCA) is the application of more than one criterion to the task of judging performance or estimating the value where various alternatives are ranked according to criteria thought to be relevant, the best alternative being chosen by calculating the extent to which it outranks others on average. The quantifiable economic rate of return would normally be included if available, and, depending on the type of project and their relevance, other criteria might include cost per beneficiary, range and scope (number of beneficiaries), distribution of benefits, ease and speed of implementation, replicability, and other systematic judgements made by experts or decision-makers. The essence of this method is that, while such methods as the CBA purport to give a categorical and definitive rule on the acceptability of a project or policy, most decision-makers are more comfortable using CBA alongside other criteria and methods, including subjective judgements (OECD, 1995; McAllister, 1995; Lichfield, 1996; Nijkamp, 1975, 1988; Voogd, 1988). The major limitation of this technique is that, unless the best alternative outweighs the others on all criteria, an implicit or explicit weighting of a subjective nature would have been attributed to the attainment of each criterion in every alternative (Buckley, 1988).

The analytic hierarchy process (AHP) is a mathematical approach to decision-making. The approach was developed in 1980 and was mainly designed to formalise the process of selecting between alternatives in a situation where full information was not available (Saaty, 1980). This method breaks down the decision or evaluation problem into parts in a hierarchical manner and makes pairwise comparisons, before building them into indicators of overall preference. However, its reliance on complex mathematical techniques renders this technique unsuitable for purposes of assessing the value of good urban design (for a detailed discussion of this technique, see Rogers & Bruen, 1995; Snell, 1997, p225).

B: Research Team Case Study Urban Design Assessments

Castle Wharf, Nottingham

Urban Design Objectives	Performance Criteria	Strengths	Weaknesses	Evaluation
1. Character	a distinct sense of place responding to local context	distinct sense of place provided by the canal and relation of the development to the canal. Successful integration of good quality new development with good quality old	some rather bland 'public' buildings i.e. the Magistrates Court on the south side of the canal	0 1 2 3 4 **5**
2. Continuity & Enclosure	clearly defined, coherent, well enclosed public space	major public space fronting the canal with a series of sub-spaces off to four enclaves, each relating well to the canal; good sense of enclosure with the scale of buildings relating well to the size of space	canal undermines enclosure but is in itself a positive feature	0 1 2 3 **4** 5
3. Quality of the Public Realm	safe, attractive and functional public space	very attractive and functional public realm, although servicing for some of the A3 uses is restricted; good feeling of safety offered by high visual accessibility and activity levels; very sunny aspect to the north of the canal enhances the lively space	public realm very poor onto Canal Street (inner ring road) which forms one boundary of the site	0 1 2 3 4 **5**
4. Ease of Movement	an accessible, well connected, pedestrian friendly environment	a very pedestrian friendly environment internally provided by almost complete pedestrianisation of the scheme and underground parking, generally well connected into the surroundings east and west with the good permeable environment giving access to the canal	poor connectivity north and south because of the inner ring road and railway line; not well connected into the city centre	0 1 2 **3** 4 5
5. Legibility	a readily understandable, easily navigable environment	very navigable and legible within the development aided by the canal and central space as key organising features	connections from Canal Street (inner ring road) to the site are less clear and to some degree the development turns its back on the city	0 1 2 3 **4** 5
6. Adaptability	flexible and adaptable public and private environments	very adaptable public realm with a range of robust sub-spaces all with removable furniture; varied private buildings suggests adaptability is a possibility	the public buildings are less articulated and adaptable	0 1 2 3 **4** 5
7. Diversity	a varied environment offering a range of uses and experiences	a good mix of uses with public courts, residential, leisure, café/restaurant, comedy club and office uses creating a rich and fine grained mix with a vital public realm day and night	south side of the canal less successful with public uses predominating and micro-climate less advantageous	0 1 2 3 **4** 5

Total Rating: 29   *0 = not at all successful   5 = very successful*

Summary:
A very successful mixed use environment that maximises on its location next to the canal and makes good use of a highly restricted site with clear edges to the north and south. The development achieves a highly permeable, attractive and vital environment with a life of its own. The commercial north side of the canal is far more successful than the 'public' south side, but overall it is clearly a successful addition to Nottingham's city centre which also opens up new possibilities along much of the city's south side.

Standard Court, Nottingham

Urban Design Objectives	Perfomance Criteria	Strengths	Weaknesses	Evaluation
1. Character	a distinct sense of place responding to local context	uses the old general hospital site and buildings to advantage, utilising high quality existing buildings and integrating the new contemporary architecture well	little sense of being special, partly because the urban design fails to give a distinct sense of place, fails to utilise the very high quality views of the Nottingham Park Estate below or to express the historical significance of the location	0 1 **2** 3 4 5
2. Continuity & Enclosure	clearly defined, coherent, well enclosed public space	one well defined central space and a number of ancillary streets/spaces; good sense of enclosure between old and new buildings		0 1 2 **3** 4 5
3. Quality of the Public Realm	safe, attractive and functional public space	well overlooked public spaces with no signs of graffiti	a rather desolate feel to the main square, largely because of the lack of activity, but also due to the very poorly detailed public realm giving a feeling of poor management and maintenance, unattractive hard landscaping and warning signs declaring the spaces to be private	0 **1** 2 3 4 5
4. Ease of Movement	an accessible, well connected, pedestrian friendly environment	a pedestrian friendly largely pedestrianised environment	site is a little disconnected from the city by the inner ring road, and with its edge of centre location is not on any major routes – hence rather isolated, high walls around south side of the space will disconnect this part of the square from the planned housing	0 1 **2** 3 4 5
5. Legibility	a readily understand-able, easily navigable environment	main square forms perceptual centre to the development and eases legibility, but only the main entrance provides a legible gateway	secondary entrances are not legible and hence development is not readily understandable, particularly the rear portions of the development; very poor legibility of the square from outside the development	0 1 **2** 3 4 5
6. Adaptability	flexible and adaptable public and private environments	main square forms an arena, clearly adaptable for a range of uses, but largely desolate when not used for special events	surrounding buildings onto main square lack active frontages and therefore can not readily be adapted to relate to the space or to change their uses	0 1 **2** 3 4 5
7. Diversity	a varied environment offering a range of uses and experiences	some mix of uses including houses, offices, residential and a bar	uses largely unrelated to each other and to the key space, with none fronting onto the space and the restaurant tucked way at the back of the scheme, the positioning of the uses rather than the mix seems to be the key problem	0 1 **2** 3 4 5

Total Rating: 14   *0 = not at all successful   5 = very successful*

Summary:
A missed opportunity to create a vital part of the urban fabric utilising the unique assets of the site. Although the site exhibits a sensitive re-use of the high quality ex-hospital buildings and includes some well designed contemporary buildings around a network of new public spaces, the isolated nature of the location and the failure to integrate key uses leaves the development feeling desolate and uncared for.

Brindleyplace, Birmingham

Urban Design Objectives	Perfomance Criteria	Strengths	Weaknesses	Evaluation
1. Character	a distinct sense of place responding to local context	relates well to the canal and to the sequence of spaces in Birmingham City Centre; creates a distinct new quarter for Birmingham – integrates older buildings well	large floor plate office blocks offer a commercial character; little fine grain detail	0 1 2 3 **4** 5
2. Continuity & Enclosure	clearly defined, coherent, well enclosed public space	a number of key public spaces – using townscape principles to provide a visually interesting network of space, main sequences are well enclosed	some undermining of spatial enclosure at the corners due to large floor plate buildings	0 1 2 3 4 **5**
3. Quality of the Public Realm	safe, attractive and functional public space	safe, attractive and functional public spaces, with private cars largely excluded; good mix of active uses to enhance public realm; high quality materials, landscape and maintenance	heavy presence of private security guards gives feeling of exclusivity	0 1 2 3 **4** 5
4. Ease of Movement	an accessible, well connected, pedestrian friendly environment	a very pedestrian friendly environment, accessible to the full range of users, well connected into the street network to the city centre, very permeable	relies on a private and controlled route through the Convention Centre	0 1 2 3 **4** 5
5. Legibility	a readily understandable, easily navigable environment	a highly legible environment, which is easy to navigate through and understand; spaces are all clearly different and unique, some landmark buildings provide external presence	most buildings lack strong character	0 1 2 3 4 **5**
6. Adaptability	flexible and adaptable public and private environments	robust public realm capable of some adaptation – although very 'designed' so unlikely to adapt to ad hoc events; colonnades surround two sides of the square for more private uses, i.e. office workers smoking	large floor plate, very commercial buildings without the fine grained divisions necessary for adaptation; some buildings lack active frontages	0 1 2 **3** 4 5
7. Diversity	a varied environment offering a range of uses and experiences	a mixed use environment, with offices, restaurants, shops, leisure and residential elements, good range of activities and mix of public and private to enliven key space	uses divided and zoned across the site, i.e. residential clearly separated; deserted at night and weekends; bars, retail, etc., mainly to serve office workers	0 1 2 3 **4** 5

Total Rating: 29   *0 = not at all successful   5 = very successful*

Summary:
Clearly a high quality, commercial environment, which is also well used and enjoyed by a wide range of users – office workers and the public (particularly visitors to the sea life centre). Wide range of uses and activities from families to office workers. A very pleasant and attractive environment, although some sense of exclusivity because of the large, obviously corporate office blocks.

Waterfront, Dudley

Urban Design Objectives	Perfomance Criteria	Strengths	Weaknesses	Evaluation
1. Character	a distinct sense of place responding to local context	use of landscaping and relationship to the canal gives a good sense of place	bland business park architecture and formal layout leave the development indistinguishable from many others of its type, poor relation of key buildings to the canal at ground floor level	0 1 **2** 3 4 5
2. Continuity & Enclosure	clearly defined, coherent, well enclosed public space	buildings form a large relatively enclosed space around the canal, but step far back from the edge; formal layout provides some continuity	large parts of the development relate poorly to the canal and form pavilions in a car park landscape; the rather forced formality breaks down around the development's edges; little variety in spatial types with just one major space centred on the canal	0 1 **2** 3 4 5
3. Quality of the Public Realm	safe, attractive and functional public space	good quality public spaces around the heart of the development onto the canal, with large areas of traffic calmed and pedestrianised space; good sense of safety and high quality soft landscaping	rather bland architecture and sense of a controlled, privatised landscape, well detailed – if rather bland – hard landscaping	0 1 2 **3** 4 5
4. Ease of Movement	an accessible, well connected, pedestrian friendly environment	internally key spaces are pedestrian friendly, although main spine roads and surrounding parking areas are not; permeable in parts	very poor connection to the surrounding area – insular business park requiring road access; not permeable beyond central areas, and large blocks reduce local connectivity; car dominated beyond central area and main streets dominated by parking	0 **1** 2 3 4 5
5. Legibility	a readily understand-able, easily navigable environment	canal provides a central marker to aid legibility, as does the formal plan and views across the development, much less clear beyond central area	in parts difficult to navigate, especially away from the central area	0 1 2 **3** 4 5
6. Adaptability	flexible and adaptable public and private environments	some use of the private realm suggests adaptability according to weather	a range of office buildings based around a formula solution; public realm dictated by the private uses, with a tendency to be insular; buildings not adaptable	0 1 **2** 3 4 5
7. Diversity	a varied environment offering a range of uses and experiences	some mixing of uses – offices/hotel/ shops/restaurants/ fitness club, but offices predominate; well used at night and over the weekend – bars/ restaurants/etc.	a formula business park environment with a limited range of uses other than office/hotel; one experience only – the office park – with little subtlety	0 1 **2** 3 4 5

Total Rating: 15 *0 = not at all successful 5 = very successful*

Summary:
A classic business park environment, although with some attempt to add value through utilising the location next to the canal, high quality soft landscaping and a formal planned framework. Successful central space around the canal, but less successful elsewhere (car dominated).

Barbirolli Square. Manchester

Urban Design Objectives	Performance Criteria	Strengths	Weaknesses	Evaluation
1. Character	a distinct sense of place responding to local context	a distinct sense of place created by a mix of old and new, making good use of the canal to create a new basin; integrates existing buildings well into the new mix	rather impersonal and over-scaled new office blocks leave the higher levels without activity	0 1 2 3 **4** 5
2. Continuity & Enclosure	clearly defined, coherent, well enclosed public space	makes good use of levels to create an enclosed space at the low level	higher level, less enclosed opening up onto a major road, the tramway and onto the GMex which relates poorly to the new square	0 1 2 3 **4** 5
3. Quality of the Public Realm	safe, attractive and functional public space	a new Pitcher & Piano café enlivens low level square, and movement along the road and in and out of buildings enlivens the space; attractive public realm with high quality materials used in the public realm; CCTV prominent	new buildings (offices, Bridgewater Hall and GMex) are all highly internalised and lack connections to the square; some poorly detailed hard landscaping	0 1 2 3 **4** 5
4. Ease of Movement	an accessible, well connected, pedestrian friendly environment	accessible and well connected to the surroundings – open on all sides of the square (although not to the north); largely pedestrianised and pedestrian friendly	some disconnection to and across the private car park between buildings; major road reduces connectivity to GMex (one pedestrian crossing and very poor dark underpass)	0 1 **2** 3 4 5
5. Legibility	a readily understand-able, easily navigable environment	easy to understand and to take in by viewing the key space from above, easily navigable to all users, including the disabled (despite level changes)	very poor underpass, and some failure to connect to surroundings undermines legibility	0 1 2 3 **4** 5
6. Adaptability	flexible and adaptable public and private environments	high level public space could offer some flexibility	public spaces not obviously adaptable, but clearly designed to be used as currently; office buildings are deep plan air conditioned buildings – not adaptable – depends for success on the bar	0 1 **2** 3 4 5
7. Diversity	a varied environment offering a range of uses and experiences	some mix with offices and Bridgewater Hall dominating and Pitcher & Piano bar at low level adding variety and life	poor connection of office buildings to the public realm – no active frontages; little variation in uses likely so limited range of experiences	0 1 2 **3** 4 5

Total Rating: 23   *0 = not at all successful   5 = very successful*

Summary:
A small development of offices and the Bridgewater Hall around a square, including the canal basin. Creates a lively public square, with clever use of levels. Less lively at the higher level, with poor connections between the buildings and the public space. Offices are clearly highly commercial and corporate in style. Building functions, including the Bridgewater Hall, are largely internalised. North side of the new space is poorly connected to the development (privatised).

Exchange Quay, Salford

Urban Design Objectives	Perfomance Criteria	Strengths	Weaknesses	Evaluation
1. Character	a distinct sense of place responding to local context	some attempt to create spaces and some public art – but of little inherent quality	a corporate international style development, with bland faceless buildings and spaces	0 **1** 2 3 4 5
2. Continuity & Enclosure	clearly defined, coherent, well enclosed public space	major buildings on a grid street structure; one main street and one key public space with some coherence	buildings sit as pavilions in space; poorly enclosed central space and little continuity to side streets; development turns its back on the surrounding area, including the canal	0 **1** 2 3 4 5
3. Quality of the Public Realm	safe, attractive and functional public space	feeling of safety within development, largely because of heavy private security presence; some use of soft landscaping and sculpture to enhance public realm	gated, obviously private development; feeling of safety diminishes at edges of development, areas around feel desolate, uncared for and unsafe; often low quality materials used in the public spaces – 'cheap and cheerful', with all around development clearly a private rather than public place; wind-tunnel problems in main public space	0 1 **2** 3 4 5
4. Ease of Movement	an accessible, well connected, pedestrian friendly environment	pedestrian friendly within confines of the development with traffic calmed main street	disconnected from the surrounding environment, cut off from public transport, reliant on cars and parking and difficult to walk beyond confines of development	0 **1** 2 3 4 5
5. Legibility	a readily understandable, easily navigable environment	navigable within heart of development	largely unnavigable around edge of development, which also makes development illegible from outside	0 1 **2** 3 4 5
6. Adaptability	flexible and adaptable public and private environments		clearly a corporate development, with little intention to offer either adaptable public or private space – dominated by large office blocks	0 **1** 2 3 4 5
7. Diversity	a varied environment offering a range of uses and experiences	some variety in office style and some mix of uses with a café and a small range of business related retail units	dominated by office uses with little variation in style or uses	0 **1** 2 3 4 5

Total Rating: 9   *0 = not at all successful 5 = very successful*

Summary:
A classic 'international style' high density car dominated development, dominated by office uses that could be anywhere. Some attempt to improve the quality of the environment through hard and soft landscaping, but little to recommend the scheme and no attempt to connect the development to its hinterland. Very heavy security guard presence confirms this is predominantly a private rather than public place.

C: Interview Pro-formas

Interview Pro-forma for Investors

Background

1. Could you briefly relate the background of your involvement with this development, covering the following main points:

   ◼ how you first got involved with the idea/project that culminated in this development

   ◼ what your initial expectations from the development were

   ◼ if these have since changed, how and why

   ◼ whether the outcome is better or worse than expected and in what way.

2. To what extent is urban design a major factor in your approach to property in general?

3. To what extent was urban design considered a major factor in your approach to the development?

Economic Benefit

1. Overall, how do you assess the prestige and reputation of this development?

2. In relation to the development's capital and rental values since its completion, please give your view on the following questions:

   ◼ Are there factors unique to this development that account for the prevailing levels of rental and capital values?

   ◼ How did these values compare with other similar projects at the time and also with your expectations at the outset?

   ◼ To what extent do you consider urban design to have a bearing on the prevailing level of these values?

3. In relation to the development's occupancy/take-up and vacancy rates, please tell me:

   ◼ the history of vacancy and take up rates in this development

   ◼ your view on the factors that account for the prevailing vacancy/take-up rates in the development

   ◼ how in your view the urban design attributes of the development account for the level of take-up or vacancy rates experienced.

4. Are you satisfied with the operational performance of this development in terms of:

   ◼ management costs

   ◼ security costs

   ◼ energy consumption.

5. How do you think the urban design has contributed to advantages or disadvantages experienced in the above areas?

6. Could you comment on the effect of the development on the following issues on a geographical scale:

   ■ local property values

   ■ place marketing

   ■ area revitalization stimulus

   ■ impact on employment.

3. Do you think that the urban design qualities of the development have led to any advantages or disadvantages in the above areas?

4. Will this effect be long-term and how will its longevity be affected by the quality of the design?

Community Benefit

1. Do you consider this place to be pleasant/attractive?

2. Is the development well integrated into its surroundings?

3. In what way do you consider this development to be contributing to the identity of, and civic pride attached to, this place or locality?

4. Do you consider this place to be lively and vibrant during the different times of the day and to what extent has the design solution affected this?

5. In what way do you consider this development to affect the social well-being of the local community?

6. In your view, does this development enhance the supply and quality of facilities and amenities at this place or locality?

7. To what extent are all sectors of the community encouraged to use the development – would they feel welcome?

8. To what extent does the design solution improve or impede the connectivity at the development to the surrounding area? Is this desirable?

Environmental Support

1. What in your view are the main impacts of this development on the local environment?

2. To what extent are environmental impacts such as energy consumption, accessibility, traffic generation, planting/ecology important in your investment decision?

3. How important do you perceive these factors to be to occupiers?

Interview Pro-forma for Developers

Background

1. Could you briefly relate the background of your involvement with this development, covering the following main points:

    - how you first got involved with the idea/project that culminated in this development

    - what your initial expectations from the development were

    - if these have since changed, how and why

    - whether the outcome is better or worse than expected and in what way.

2. To what extent is urban design a factor in your approach to development in general?

3. To what extent was urban design considered a factor in your approach to the development?

4. Has this development been the winner of any awards in respect of the quality of its design? Who awarded it and for what particular strengths?

Economic Benefit

1. Overall, how do you assess the prestige and the reputation of this development?

2. Does the development reflect the image you wish to establish for your business and developments?

3. What factors peculiar to the urban design of this development might have influenced its prestige and reputation?

4. In relation to the development's capital and rental values since its completion, please give your view on the following questions:

    - Are there factors unique to this development that account for the prevailing levels of rental and capital values?

    - How did these values compare with other similar projects at the time and also with your expectations at the outset?

    - To what extent do you consider urban design to have a bearing on the prevailing level of these values?

5. In relation to the environment created, how typical or untypical did the procurement of this development turn out to be judged on the basis of the following factors and why:

    - production costs

    - infrastructure costs

    - duration and cost of planning approval process

    - requirements of the planning authority

    - design costs

    - ease of finding investors?

6. Could you comment on the effect of the development on the following issues on a geographical scale:

   - local property values

   - place marketing

   - area revitalization stimulus

   - impact on employment.

7. Do you think that the urban design qualities of the development have led to any advantages or disadvantages in the above areas?

Community Benefit

1. Do you consider this place to be pleasant/attractive?

2. Is the development well integrated into its surroundings?

3. In what way do you consider this development to be contributing to the identity of, and civic pride attached to, this place or locality?

4. Do you consider this place to be lively and vibrant during the different times of the day and to what extent has the design solution affected this?

5. In what way do you consider this development to affect the social well-being of the local community?

6. In your view, does this development enhance the supply and quality of facilities and amenities at this place or locality, is that important?

7. To what extent are all sectors of the community encouraged to use the development – would they feel welcome?

8. To what extent does the design solution improve or impede the connectivity at the development to the surrounding area? Is this desirable?

Environmental Support

1. What in your view are the main impacts of this development on the local environment?

2. To what extent did environmental impacts such as energy consumption, accessibility, traffic generation, planting/ecology inform the urban design concept?

3. Are these factors important to you and your clients?

4. Does the development have a BREEAM rating?

5. How have you addressed the question of pedestrian and vehicular accessibility to the site?

6. How was the urban design solution affected by that?

7. Do you consider this development to have had a significant impact in the locality in terms of traffic generation? Please explain your views.

8. Do you consider the natural environment to be sufficiently integrated in this development? How in your view have the design features of this place achieved that?

Interview Pro-forma for Designers

Background

1. Could you briefly relate the background of your involvement with this development, covering the following main points:

    ■ how you first got involved with the idea/project that culminated in this development

    ■ what your initial expectations from the development were

    ■ if these have since changed, how and why

    ■ whether the outcome is better or worse than expected and in what way.

2. To what extent is urban design a major factor in your approach to development in general?

3. To what extent was urban design considered a major factor in your approach to the development?

4. Has this development been the winner of any awards in respect of the quality of its design? Who awarded it and for what particular strengths?

Economic Viability

1. Overall, how do you assess the prestige and reputation of development? What factors peculiar to the urban design of this development might have influenced its prestige and reputation?

2. How did the concept respond to the issues of:

    ■ management costs

    ■ security costs

    ■ energy consumption

    ■ productivity of occupiers/organisation

    ■ popularity with retail and restaurant outlets and their customers

    ■ health and satisfaction of workforce?

3. In relation to the environment created, how typical or untypical did the procurement of this development turn out to be judged on the basis of the following factors and why:

    ■ production costs

    ■ infrastructure costs

    ■ duration and cost of planning approval process

    ■ planning gain required by the planning authorities

    ■ design costs?

Community Benefit

1. Is the development well integrated into its surroundings?

2. In what way do you consider this development to be contributing to the identity of, and civic pride attached to, this place or locality?

3. Do you consider this place to be lively and vibrant during the different times of the day and to what extent has the design solution affected this?

4. In what way do you consider this development to affect the social well-being of the local community?

5. How accessible is the development – both within and across it, and in its connections to the surrounding area?

6. In what way do you consider the urban design solution to have improved or impeded the connectivity of this place to the surrounding area?

7. In your view, does this development enhance the supply and quality of facilities and amenities at this place or locality?

8. To what extent was personal safety considered in the design of the development and how did this inform the urban design solution?

Environmental Support

1. What in your view are the main impacts of this development on the local environment?

2. To what extent did environmental impacts such as energy consumption, accessibility, traffic generation, planting/ecology inform the urban design concept?

3. Are these factors important to you and your clients?

4. Does the development have a BREEAM rating?

5. Was energy consumption a factor considered during the design development?

6. Do you consider the natural environment to be sufficiently integrated in this development? How in your view have the design features of this place achieved that?

Interview Pro-forma for Occupiers

Background

1. Could you briefly relate the background of your involvement with this development, covering the following main points:

   ■ how you first got involved with the idea/project that culminated in this development

   ■ what your initial expectations from the development were

   ■ if these have since changed, how and why

   ■ whether the outcome is better or worse than expected and in what way.

2. To what extent is urban design a factor in your approach to choosing office space in general?

3. To what extent was urban design considered a factor in your approach to choosing this development?

Economic Viability

1. In relation to the development's rental values since its completion, please give your view on the following questions:

   ■ How satisfied are you with the current rental values you are paying/capital values? If not please explain your concerns.

   ■ How did these values compare with other similar projects at the time of moving to this development and how have they varied since?

   ■ Are there factors unique to this development that account for the prevailing levels of rental and capital values?

   ■ To what extent do you consider urban design to have a bearing on the prevailing level of these values?

   ■ Would you consider there to be a relationship between the cost of this development, especially investment in urban design, and the prevailing level of these values?

2. Overall, how do you assess the prestige and reputation of this development? What factors peculiar to the urban design of this development might have influenced its prestige and reputation?

3. Does the development complement your corporate image – if so, in what way?

4. Are you satisfied with the operational performance of this development in terms of:

   ■ management costs

   ■ security costs

   ■ energy consumption

   ■ productivity of organisation

   ■ health and satisfaction of workforce?

5. How do you think the urban design has contributed to advantages or disadvantages experienced in the above areas?

Community Benefit

1. Do you consider this place to be pleasant/attractive?

2. Is the development well integrated into its surroundings?

3. In what way do you consider this development to be contributing to the identity of, and civic pride attached to, this place or locality?

4. Do you consider this place to be lively and vibrant during the different times of the day and to what extent has the design solution affected this?

5. In what way do you consider this development to affect the social well-being of the local community?

6. To what extent do your clients/customers feel welcome while visiting this place and would all kinds of people feel welcome here?

7. Do you think the design features of this development play any role in the above?

8. How accessible is the development – both within and across it, and in its connections to the surrounding area?

9. In what way do you consider the quality of the urban design solution to have improved or impeded the connectivity of this place to the area?

10. Do you feel safe while working in this place and what factors account for your feeling during the day and night?

11. In your view, does this development enhance the supply and quality of facilities and amenities at this place or locality?

12. Which aspects of the development, outside your office space, do you most enjoy and use?

Environmental Support

1. What in your view are the main impacts of this development on the local environment?

2. How accessible is the development and has the urban design solution affected the travel patterns of your workforce?

3. Do you consider the natural environment to be sufficiently integrated in this development? How in your view have the design features of this place achieved that?

4. To what extent are environmental impacts such as energy consumption, accessibility, traffic generation and planting/ecology important in your decision to locate here?

Interview Pro-forma for Planning & Economic Development Officers

Background

1. Could you briefly relate the background of your involvement with this development, covering the following main points:

   - how you first got involved with the idea/project that culminated in this development

   - what your initial expectations from the development were

   - if these have since changed, how and why

   - whether the outcome is better or worse than expected and in what way.

2. To what extent is urban design a factor in your approach to development in general?

3. To what extent was urban design considered a factor in your approach to the development?

Economic Viability

1. What factors peculiar to the urban design of this development might have influenced its prestige and reputation?

2. In relation to the development's capital and rental values since its completion, please give your view on the following questions:

   - Are there factors unique to this development that account for the prevailing levels of rental and capital values?

   - How did these values compare with other similar projects at the time and also with your expectations at the outset?

   - To what extent do you consider urban design to have a bearing on the prevailing level of these values?

3. In relation to the environment created, how typical or untypical did the procurement of this development turn out to be judged on the basis of the following factors and why:

   - infrastructure costs

   - duration and cost of planning approval process

   - planning gain

   - ease of finding investors?

   Which of the above were borne by the private and which by the public sector?

4. Could you comment on the effect of the development on the following issues on a geographical scale:

   - local property values

   - place marketing

   - area revitalisation stimulus

   - impact on employment.

5. Do you think that the urban design qualities of the development have led to any advantages or disadvantages in the above areas?

6. Will this effect be long-term and how will its longevity be affected by the quality of the design?

Community Benefit

1. Do you consider this place to be pleasant/attractive?

2. Is the development well integrated into its surroundings?

3. In what way do you consider this development to be contributing to the identity of, and civic pride attached to, this place or locality?

4. Do you consider this place to be lively and vibrant during the different times of the day and to what extent has the design solution affected this?

5. In what way do you consider this development to affect the social well-being of the local community?

6. How accessible is the development – both within and across it, and in its connections to the surrounding area?

7. In what way do you consider the urban design solution to have improved or impeded the connectivity of this place to the environs?

8. In your view, does this development enhance the supply and quality of facilities and amenities at this place or locality?

9. To what extent are all sectors of the community encouraged to use the development – would they feel welcome?

10. To what extent does the design solution improve or impede the connectivity at the development to the surrounding area? Is this desirable?

Environmental Support

1. What in your view are the main impacts of this development on the local environment?

2. To what extent did environmental impacts such as energy consumption, accessibility, traffic generation, planting/ecology inform the urban design concept?

3. How do you assess the impact of this development on pedestrian and vehicular access at this place/locality?

4. What design features do you think account for the effect of development on local accessibility?

5. Do you consider this development to have had a significant impact in the locality in terms of traffic generation?

6. Are there significant effects of this development on the average length and duration of journeys to work in this locality? Which aspects of its design might account for that?

7. Do you consider the natural environment to be sufficiently integrated in this development? How in your view have the design features of this place achieved that?

8. Was energy consumption a factor considered when giving planning permission?

Interview Pro-forma for Everyday Users

Background

1. How frequently do you come here?

2. What is the main reason for your visits?

Economic Viability

1. In what way would you consider this development to be of economic benefit to the users and the local community at large?

2. Do you think that the urban design qualities of the development generate any benefits? Please explain.

Community Benefit

1. Do you consider this place to be pleasant/attractive?

2. Is the development well integrated into its surroundings?

3. In what way do you consider this development to be contributing to the identity of, and civic pride attached to, this place or locality?

4. Do you consider this place to be lively and vibrant during the different times of the day and to what extent has the design solution affected this?

5. In what way do you consider this development to affect the social well-being of the local community in the area?

6. To what extent do you feel welcome while visiting this place and would all kinds of people feel welcome here?

7. Do you think the design features of this development play any role in the way you feel about this place?

8. How accessible is the development – both within and across it, and in its connections to the surrounding area?

9. In what way do you consider the quality of the urban design solution to have improved or impeded the connectivity of this place to the surrounding environment?

10. Do you feel safe while working in or visiting this place and what factors account for it during the day and night?

11. In your view, does this development enhance the supply and quality of facilities and amenities at this place or locality?

12. Which aspects of the development do you most enjoy and use?

Environmental Support

1. How do you assess the impact of this development on pedestrians and vehicle access at this place/locality?

2. Do you consider this development to have had a significant impact in the locality in terms of traffic generation? Please explain your views.

3. Do you consider the natural environment to be sufficiently integrated in this development? How in your view have the design features of this place achieved that?

Bibliography

Adams D (1994) *Urban Planning and the Development Process,* London, UCL Press

Alexander C (1977) *A Pattern language,* Oxford, Oxford University Press

Asabere P, Hachey G & Grubaugh S (1989) 'Architecture, historic zoning, and the value of homes' *Journal of Real Estate Finance and Economics,* Vol.2, pp181–95.

Bannock G, Baxter R & Davis E (1998) *Dictionary of Economics,* London, Profile Books

Begg D, Fischer S & Dornbusch R (1994) *Economics,* 4th Edition, London, McGraw-Hill

Bentley I, Alcock A, Murrain P, McGlynn S & Smith G (1985) *Responsive Environments: A Manual for Designers,* Oxford, Butterworth Architecture

Bourassa S, Neutze M & Strong A (1994) *Leasehold Policies and Land Use Planning in Canberra,* Canberra, ANU Research School of Social Sciences

Britton W (1989) *The Economic, Efficient, and Effective Management of Public Authority Landed Estates,* London, School of Surveying, Kingston University

Buckley M (1988) 'Multicriteria evaluation: measures, manipulation and measuring' *Environment and Planning B: Planning and Design,* Vol.15, No.1, pp55–64

Carmona M. (1996) 'Controlling Urban Design – Part 1: A Possible Renaissance?' *Journal of Urban Design,* Vol.1, No.1, pp47–73

Carmona M (1998) 'Design Control – Bridging the Professional Divide, Part 2: A New Consensus' *Journal of Urban Design,* Vol.3, No.3, pp331–358

Carmona M (1999) 'Controlling the Design of Private Sector Residential Development: An Agenda for Improving Practice' *Environment and Planning B: Planning and Design,* Vol.26, pp807–833

Cheshire P (2000) 'Building on brown fields: the long-term price we pay' *Planning in London,* Vol.33, pp34–35

Cheshire P & Shepherd S (1994) 'On the Price of Land and the value of Amenities' *Economica,* Vol.62, pp247–67

Clarke L (1992) *Building Capitalism,* London, Routledge

Combs J, Kirkpatrick R, Shogren J & Herriges J (1993) 'Matching grants and public goods: a closed ended contingent valuation experiment' *Public Finance Quarterly,* Vol.21, No.2, pp178–95

Cowan R (1995) *The Cities Design Forgot,* London, Urban Initiatives

Cowan R (2000) Placecheck, *A Users' Guide,* London, Urban Design Alliance

Department of National Heritage (DNH), English Heritage, and The Royal Institution of Chartered Surveyors (1996) *The Value of Conservation: A Literature Review of the Economic and Social Value of Cultural Built Heritage,* London, RICS

DETR & CABE (2000) By Design, *Urban Design in the Planning System: Towards Better Practice,* London, Thomas Telford

DoE (1997) *Planning Policy Guidance Note 1: General Policy and Principles,* London, The Stationery Office

Doiron J, Shilling J & Sirmans C (1992) 'Do market rents reflect the value of special building features? The case of office atriums' *The Journal of Real Estate Research,* Vol.7, No.2, pp147–155

Duffy F (1999) 'British Airways at Waterside: A new model office?' *Architectural Research Quarterly,* Vol.3, No.2, pp125 – 140

Eccles T (1996) 'The professional concept of value within the built environment: a conceptual critique' *Environment By Design,* Vol.1, No.1, pp39 – 52

Eppli M & Tu C (1999) *Valuing the New Urbanism: The Impact of the New Urbanism on Prices of Single Family Houses,* Washington DC, Urban Land Institute

Frey H (1999) *Designing the City: Towards a More Sustainable Urban Form,* London, E & FN Spon

Gummer J (1994) *DoE News Release 713, More Quality in Town & Country,* London, DoE

Guy S (1998) 'Developing alternatives: energy, offices and the environment' *International Journal of Urban and Regional Research,* Vol.22, No.2, pp264 – 282

Hebbert M (1998) *London: More by Fortune than Design,* Chichester, Wiley

Hough D & Kratz C (1983) 'Can "good" architecture meet the market test?' *Journal of Urban Economics,* Vol.14, pp40 – 54

Jeffrey D & Reynolds G (1999) 'Planners, architects, the public, and aesthetics factor analysis or preferences for infill development', *Journal of Architectural and Planning Research,* Vol.16, No.4, pp271 – 288

Lang J (1994) *Urban Design, The American Experience,* New York, Van Nostrand Reinhold

Lichfield N (1996) *Community Impact Evaluation,* London, UCL Press

Lipsey R & Chrystal K (1995) *An Introduction To Positive Economics,* Oxford, Oxford University Press

Llewelyn-Davies (2000) *Urban Design Compendium,* London, English Partnerships and the Housing Corporation

Lock D (1993) 'The developer and the urban design process' *Urban Design Quarterly,* April, pp28–31

Loe K (1999) *The Value of Architecture – Context and Current Thinking,* RIBA Future Studies series, London, RIBA

Loukaitou-Sideris A & Banerjee T (1998) *Urban Design Downtown, Poetics and Politics of Form, Berkeley,* University of California Press

Lynch K (1960) *The Image of the City,* Cambridge, MA, MIT Press

Madanipour A (1996) *Design of Urban Space, An Inquiry into a Socio-spatial Process,* Wiley, Chichester

McAllister D (1995) *Evaluation in Environmental Planning: Assessing Environmental, Social, Economic, and Political Trade-Offs,* Cambridge, MA, MIT Press.

McGlynn S & Murrain P (1994) 'The politics of urban design' *Planning Practice and Research,* Vol.9, No.3, pp311–319

Morton R & Jagger D (1995) *Design and the Economics of Building,* London, E & FN Spon

Nijkamp P (1975) 'A multicriteria analysis for project evaluation' *Papers for the Regional Science Association,* Vol.35, pp28–33

Nijkamp P, Rietvold P & Voogd H (1991) *Multicriteria Analysis in Physical Planning,* Amsterdam, North Holland

Organisation for Economic Co-operation and Development (1995) *The Economic Appraisal of Environmental Projects And Policies: A Practical Guide,* Paris, OECD

Pearce D & Markandya A (1991) *Blueprint for a Green Economy,* London, Earthscan

Parfect M & Power G (1997) *Planning for Urban Quality: Urban Design in Towns and Cities,* London, Routledge

Property Council of Australia (1999) *The Design Dividend,* Canberra, PCA National Office

Punter J & Carmona M (1997) *The Design Dimension of Planning, Theory, Content and Best Practice for Design Policies,* London, E & FN Spon

Rabeneck A (1999) 'Joined-up thinking?' *RIBA Journal,* November, pp27–28

RFAC (1994) *What Makes a Good Building? An Inquiry by the Royal Fine Art Commission,* London, HMSO

RICS & DoE (1996) *Quality of Urban Design: A Study on the Involvement of Private Property Decision-makers in Urban Design,* London, Royal Institution of Chartered Surveyors and Department of the Environment

Rogers, M & Bruen M (1995) 'Non monetary based decision-aid techniques in environmental impact assessment - an overview' *Municipal Engineering,* June, pp98–103

Rouse R (1998), *'The seven clamps of urban design', Planning,* No.1293, pp18-19

Rudlin D & Falk N (1999) *Building the 21st Century Home: The Sustainable Urban Neighbourhood,* Oxford, The Architectural Press

Saaty T (1980) *The Analytic Hierarchy Process,* New York, Mc Graw-Hill

Smith S (1989) *Tourism Analysis: A Handbook,* Harlow, Longman Scientific and Technical

Snell M (1997) *Cost–Benefit Analysis for Engineers and Planners,* London, Thomas Telford

Stanlake G (1980) *Introductory Economics,* 6th Edition, Aylesbury, Longman

Summerson J (1978) *Georgian London,* London, Penguin

Tibbalds F (1988) 'Urban design: Tibbalds offers the prince his ten commandments', *The Planner,* Vol.74 No.12, p1 (mid-month supplement)

Urban Design Group (1994) *Urban Design Source Book,* Abingdon Oxon, UDG

Urban Task Force (1999) *Towards an Urban Renaissance,* London, E&FN Spon

Urban Villages Forum (1995) *Economics of Urban Villages,* London, Urban Villages Forum

Vandell K & Lane J (1989) 'The economics of architecture and urban design: some preliminary findings' *Journal of the American Real Estate and Urban Economics Association,* Vol.17, No.2, pp235–260

Verhage R & Needham B (1997) 'Negotiating about the residential environment: it is not only money that matters' *Urban Studies,* Vol.34, No.12, pp2053–2086

Voogd H (1988) 'Multicriteria evaluation: measures, manipulation and meaning: a reply' *Environment and Planning B: Planning and Design,* Vol.15, No.1, pp65–72

Willis K, Garrod G, Saunders C & Whitby M (1993) 'Assessing methodologies to value the benefits of environmentally sensitive areas' *Countryside Change Unit Working Paper 39,* Newcastle upon Tyne, Department of Agricultural Economics and Food Marketing, University of Newcastle upon Tyne

Worpole K (1999) *The Value of Architecture – Design, Economy and the Architectural Imagination,* RIBA Future Studies series, London, RIBA